DARK CONTRACTS

Breaking the Nex of Narcissistic and Psychopathic Control

By Deirdre Rolfe

"For every soul who learned to walk away with a confused and shattered heart but with eyes wide open."

FOREWORD

There are wounds so invisible they leave no bruise, scar or evidence, just an ache felt so deeply, it's palpable. It's a sign, your abuse lives in the invisible and you have been haunted by the dark ghost, hijacked by the person who was meant to love you.

This book is born from that ache of your inner knowing, where the real, truth lives. It gives a voice to the unspoken aftermath of dark triad relationships that don't just leave you with broken bones but with a broken compass. The kind of bonds that masquerade as love yet slowly erase your voice, your clarity, even the sense of who you are. That defining moment of awakening is both cognitive revelation and existential rupture. The mind once fogged sharpens into terrifying clarity. Patterns that once felt disjointed now crystallize into a map of systematic dismantling. The intuitive dissonance and the body's protest was never delusion, it was data. This is where the why, forces us to dig deeper into the neuropsychology of trauma bonding, the psycholinguistics of manipulation and deception and the somatic imprint of prolonged betrayal. This moment is the threshold where you chose to disintegrate or self-author while holding both the full weight of your collapse and the fight of your resurrection.

DARK CONTRACTS BY DEIRDRE ROLFE

For over three decades I have sat across from people who could not name or fully articulate their pain. People who blamed themselves for the emotional chaos they had been conditioned to survive. People who told their stories not in defiance but in whispers because they still feared being disbelieved. The abuse was designed to be unbelievable. Dark triad individuals are covert, strategic, performative, and image focused. They craft a dual reality, one version for public consumption; charming, generous, misunderstood and one version behind closed doors; controlling, cruel, calculated and emotionally carnivorous. They feed off your confusion while wearing a mask of concern. When a survivor tries to tell the truth, it often sounds implausible even to them. Just like the survivors of the holocaust who endured unimaginable atrocities, it was designed to be too much for anyone to comprehend and that was its power. Dark triad abuse is a slow-drip vampirism nursing off the veins of its victims and it happens in the invisible, it happens while you stay, asleep. It doesn't look like what people expect. There are no bruises, but there are holes in the psyche and thousands of micro erased boundaries.

The abuser was charming in public, generous to friends, polite to your parents but a ghost, vampire, tyrant, devil, deceptive or interrogator in private. So, when you finally say: *"They manipulated me, controlled me, erased me,"* you're often met with: *"But they were always so nice!"* That's how survivors learn to self-silence because speaking feels like digging their own grave in public opinion. Psychopaths and narcissists flip the narrative before you can escape it. They plant seeds early so by the time you begin falling apart, you've already been painted as the problem. You feel crazy because that's the role they pre-cast for you. When you react (out of betrayal, heartbreak, or trauma), they point and say: *"See? That's who they really are."* You become the proof of your own undoing.

Chaos is not linear, and storytelling requires coherence. There is no clear beginning or end. One day you're loved, the next ignored. One week idealized, the next erased. So, survivors default to silence, not because they don't remember but because they don't know how to make it, make sense to people who weren't inside it. For many survivors, even after leaving, the abuser still controls the narrative, so the silence becomes a shield, but it also becomes a cage. Speaking your story restores coherence to a mind fractured by manipulation.

Every time a survivor tells their story without being shamed or dismissed, a part of them reattaches to reality. The

DARK CONTRACTS BY DEIRDRE ROLFE

fog clears. The inner child who was silenced learns: *"We are no longer invisible, dismissed or abandoned."* Telling the truth isn't just cathartic, it is neurologically reparative. It calms the nervous system. It grounds the self. It begins the rewiring from shame to sovereignty, enmeshment to individuation. If you are witnessing a survivor speak, know this: Your belief is medicine. Your presence is reparative attachment. You don't need to fix their story just listen, be, hold space and *witness it fully*. Their nervous system is primed to scan for threat, be the safe calm, the eye in the needle of the storm, so they can breathe and find themselves. Every survivor needs someone to say *"I believe you. You make sense. And you never deserved any of it, YOU NEVER DESERVED ANY OF IT."*

Dark Contracts: Breaking the Nex of Narcissistic and Psychopathic Control was written for them and for you. This is not a manual, it is a mirror, a ritual, a map, a decoder ring, a compass and a reclamation. Here, we name the unnameable: the Nex.

The psychic web woven by dark triad personalities, narcissists, psychopaths, and Machiavellians who entangle others in silent contracts of control, guilt, and energetic theft. We expose the patterns, decode the strategies, and most importantly, light the path out. You will not find simplistic calls for forgiveness here. You will not be shamed for your rage, your confusion, or your fantasies of revenge. Instead, you will find language for your wounds and rituals for your return. If you are reading this, you already survived. Now, let us break the contract, and rise.

> *"You are a child of the universe no less than the trees and the stars; you have a right to be here ..."*

Desiderata, Max Ehrmann

Deirdre Rolfe xx

ABOUT THE AUTHOR

Deirdre Rolfe is the author of Dark Contracts: Breaking the Nex of Narcissistic and Psychopathic Control, a groundbreaking work exploring the hidden psychological agreements that entrap trauma survivors in cycles of emotional bondage. She is also the author of You Are as Sick as Your Secrets: Trauma Understands Trauma (A Memoir), a powerful examination of secrecy, money, power, and healing. Deirdre Rolfe is a psychotherapist, writer and trauma recovery specialist with over 30 years of experience working at the intersection of psychology, philosophy, and spiritual reclamation.

Her work is founded in a rare integration of evidence-based clinical frameworks and metaphoric, symbolic, somatic rituals designed to restore power, presence, and personal sovereignty. She is the creator of The TR6 Model, a powerful therapeutic tool that maps the path from trauma to embodied embitterment and the developer of The Trauma Code Deck, a therapeutic 96 card system that provides an innovative resource for shadow work, inner child healing, and narrative transformation. Deirdre is known for her fierce compassion, her unapologetic truth-telling, and her ability to hold space for both scientific rigor, existential digging and deep spiritual knowing. Dark Contracts is her signature work, an offering for those who have been silenced by psychological abuse pertaining to Narcissistic, Psychopathic personality types and are now ready to reclaim the pen.

    She lives in the forest with her partner, Col and their four beloved dogs, where she continues to work with clients and mentors fellow therapists. Her deepest passion lies in sharing the knowledge she's cultivated through decades of lived and professional experience and witnessing the profound transformation of those who dare to thrive.

Copyright © 2025 Deirdre Rolfe
All rights reserved.

No part of this publication may be reproduced, distributed, or transmitted in any form or by any means, including photocopying, recording, or other electronic or mechanical methods, without the prior written permission of the author, except in the case of brief quotations embodied in critical reviews and certain other non-commercial uses permitted by copyright law. This book and all its original content, including concepts, frameworks, terminology (e.g. "The Nex," "TR6 Model," "Dark Contracts"), therapeutic exercises, and rituals are the intellectual property of Deirdre Rolfe and may not be adapted, taught, replicated, or distributed without express written consent. This work is based on the author's original clinical perspective and is intended for educational and therapeutic insight. It is not a substitute for professional medical or psychological care.

For permissions, inquiries, or rights requests, please contact:
Deirdre Rolfe
61 412106496
Rolfe90@hotmail.com
www.counselloroncall.com.au

TABLE OF CONTENTS

Chapter One: The Nex 1

Chapter Two: Dark Contracts 28

Chapter Three: The War Against Your Inner Truth 44

Chapter Four: The Collapse of Identity 52

Chapter Five: The Dark Lure of Power Reversal 59

Chapter Six: Soul Theft 65

Chapter Seven: The War Between Knowing and Denial 72

Chapter Eight: Ghosted by the Living 78

Chapter Nine: The False Resurrection 86

Chapter Ten: The Shadow you Stayed for 95

Epilogue/Conclusion: You were never broken 103

References: & Book Recommendations 107

Acknowledgments

To the survivors: Your stories shaped every page. Your courage, even in silence, lives in every line of this book. To the clients I've worked with over three decades, thank you for letting me walk beside you in truth, your deep, personal, brave sharing and allowing me to witness your rise. To the narcissists and psychopaths on my own path who mistook my kindness for weakness and my love for permission; you were the fire wood, this book is the flame. Finally, to the younger version of me who didn't yet have words for what she felt, this book is for you. I know how much love and family means to you, you were so brave to leave.

Chapter One: The Nex

"Some bonds are not relationships. They are contracts: silent, coercive, and concealed. The Nex is the architecture of control disguised as connection."

There are forms of entrapment so sophisticated they do not require chains. They need only intimacy without accountability, closeness without conscience and promises built on persuasion rather than principle. These entanglements do not appear dangerous at first glance. They appear profound, fated and magnetic. That illusion is by design.

The Nex is a term I use to describe this invisible architecture, a system, a web of unconscious contracts woven through the dynamics of emotional, psychological, financial, and even spiritual exploitation. Unlike overt abuse, which is explicit and observable, the Nex is built from implicit. The implicit are all the things in the invisible; unspoken agreements, unconscious dynamics, underlying expectations and unspoken rules that bind. This space or Nex is the unreality or chaos where you no longer respond to life you react to theirs. You don't see it, but it is mirrored in your body, while your intuition is on mute. It thrives in implication, suggestion, and emotional conditioning. It binds through what is unsaid.

The Nex is not a metaphor. It is a living psychological structure: a system of unconscious agreements, forged not with informed consent but through manipulation, projection, and trauma-responsive acquiescence. It is the signature of control-based personalities, especially those who embody traits of narcissism, machiavellianism, and psychopathy, collectively known in psychological literature as the dark triad. While the Nex is often described as a web or trap it is just as accurately understood as a relational system, a living, reactive matrix shaped by emotional contagion and nervous system synchrony. In any emotional or relational system, each participant is not separate but interdependent. As in family systems or network theory, what affects one node affects the whole. When one person in the Nex is dysregulated, angry, manipulative, avoidant or dissociated, their nervous system begins unconsciously broadcasting signals into the field. The other person, especially if they are trauma-conditioned to over-attune, begins downloading that emotional content as if it were their own. This is more than empathy, it is neurobiology.

Our vagus nerve and neuron systems are constantly syncing, scanning, and adapting to the emotional states of those around us. Within the Nex, this results in emotional contagion, where the victim absorbs not only the moods, but the core distortions of the abuser. The result is a looping closed system where no clarity can arise, only reaction. Dark triad personalities learn, sometimes intuitively and sometimes through conscious study, that language is leverage. They weaponize language in the delivery of innuendo, tone, calculated prolonged pauses and insinuations to destabilize and dominate. The temperature is abrupt, but it is delivered in a sugar-coated covering, just to make swallowing easier. The message is clear, stay in line or suffer the consequences. They know that if they can control the emotional climate, they can reshape your perception of yourself. They watch. They test. They adapt.

The DSM-5-TR; (Diagnostic and statistical manual of mental disorders, fifth edition, text revision}, does not have a formal diagnosis for "psychopath" or "sociopath", instead, it includes antisocial personality disorder, under which both psychopathy and sociopathy are often discussed in clinical and forensic settings. Narcissistic Personality Disorder however is a distinct and separate diagnosis in the DSM-5-TR. Here's a descriptive comparison of the three, drawing from the DSM-5-TR criteria and supported by clinical literature:

Narcissist

Core Features: grandiosity, self-importance, and a need for excessive admiration. Lack of empathy, difficulty recognizing or caring about others' feelings, entitlement, arrogance, and exploitative relationships. Envious of others or believes others are envious of them, their identity is fragile, despite outward confidence. They are emotionally reactive when criticized or not admired, feels shame, humiliation, or an emptiness beneath their inflated self-view, and they use people for validation, seeks supply (attention, admiration) but may discard others when no longer useful.

Psychopath

Core Features: (based on the Hare Psychopathy Checklist, which complements DSM criteria) They have traits of callousness, shallow affect, lack of remorse or guilt. They are manipulative, deceptive, and superficially charming, highly calculated and emotionally detached. They show no genuine emotional bonds. Others are objects or pawns as they act cold, unemotional and show a lack of fear or anxiety. They don't experience guilt, show any physiological reactivity to harm caused. They mimic empathy or charm to manipulate and engage in predatory behavior, often with long-term planning.

Sociopath

Core Features: impulsive, reckless, and easily agitated, disregard for social norms and laws. They can form attachments to certain individuals or groups and are likely to engage in reactive aggression or violence. They are prone to rage, frustration, and erratic emotional outbursts and may feel loyalty or possessiveness over select people but still violate their boundaries. They have poor impulse control makes relationships chaotic, less strategic than psychopaths and more reactive and emotionally unstable. (DSM-5-TR Category American Psychiatric Association. (2022). Diagnostic and statistical manual of mental disorders (5th ed., text rev.). American Psychiatric Publishing.)

The common links all dark triads have and what one might describe as the shared thread are: a deep wound of shame or abandonment, a refusal to process vulnerability, a compensatory false self-driven by image, control, or seduction, a lack of internal moral compass, they navigate the world by manipulating others instead, an inability to truly attach, people become tools, mirrors, or threats, a dissociation from remorse emotionally or neurologically. (Kernberg, 1992; Millon et al., 2004; Hare, 1999; Kiehl, 2006; Ronningstam, 2005).

This is why all dark triad individuals share patterns of: splitting, a form of black-and-white thinking, idealization followed by devaluation, projection attributing disowned feelings to others, triangulation creating rivalry or confusion between people to maintain control, shame avoidance masked as arrogance, charm, or moral superiority, empathy deficits due to either neurological underdevelopment or learned indifference (e.g., amygdala hypoactivity in psychopathy; see Kiehl, 2006).

A Narcissist may just be a Narcissist, but a Psychopath or Sociopath often includes narcissism as part of their profile. They all share the trait of self or false self-preservation. They don't just protect themselves from others. They protect themselves from *themselves*. They sense the void within so rather than entering it, they build fortresses of defence. Within those walls, they exile the parts of themselves that once felt human, soft or real. They create a false self and that false self becomes their armour, flawless, admired and immune to criticism. Rather than metabolize their shadow, they weaponize it by projecting their inner chaos onto others.

What they cannot tolerate inside, they project outward: you're the selfish one, you're the liar, you abandoned me, you made me do this. This is disowned pain in action. Projection is not just manipulation, it is survival for a psyche that cannot risk collapse. The more chaotic their internal world, the more controlling they become in the external one. They manage emotions by managing people. They regulate self-worth by dominating attention. They avoid authentic intimacy because intimacy requires vulnerability, and vulnerability would force them to face the wound. So, they seduce, love-bomb, mimic closeness, but never actually attach. Many dark triads grew up in enmeshed, abusive, or neglectful homes. Their nervous system learned early that powerlessness is dangerous, attachment is conditional, and feelings are a liability. So, they create the same environment for others that they once endured, not consciously, but because that's what feels safe. In Jungian terms, they live in a closed circuit of the unintegrated shadow. In Lucanian terms, they are forever trying to fill the lack in the symbolic order, trying to become whole through external reinforcement but it never works, because wholeness doesn't come from control. It comes from surrender, and they are terrified of surrender. Dark triads defences are brilliant adaptations to unendurable pain, but those same defences become the very cage they cannot escape and that's why healing rarely happens.

    The healing would require the one thing they fear most, looking inward and feeling it all. Dark triads don't or more precisely *can't* change, not just because healing threatens the death of the false self but because many of them fail to succeed in life in the grandiose way they envisioned. The longer this failure persists, the more intolerable it becomes to face the gap between who they are and who they pretend to be because to change would require facing profound shame, impotence and existential failure, the very things their personality structure was built to deny. Sociopaths, narcissists, and psychopaths often can't change not simply because it would mean the death of the false self but because change requires facing a life unlived. To face that truth, to admit they are neither special nor successful in the way they demand, is to confront the original shame they were built to escape. So instead of changing, they calcify. They cling harder to delusion. Their inability to evolve becomes a survival strategy, not a flaw of willpower. As Millon (2004) and Kohut (1971) observed, the narcissistic structure is intolerant of failure. When success doesn't materialize, they don't grow they disintegrate. Change then, is not a possibility. It is a threat to the only self they believe can survive. Behind the false self is a child who was never allowed to exist as they truly were. It's not simply insecurity, it's a void where authentic selfhood should have been formed, replaced instead by a performance built to survive, neglect, control, shame or abuse. The child is no longer reachable and in many cases, it is completely disowned replaced by the false self that cannot tolerate vulnerability. (Winnicott 1965) (kohut1971) (Kernberg 1975) Miller (1981) Mate 2003).

    This explains why and how these dark contracts get signed. Even the strongest sense of self can be worn down through repetition, confusion and psychological seduction. Not by force, but through what social psychologist Robert Cialdini (2001) calls the principles of persuasion which includes, authority, social proof, consistency, liking, scarcity, and reciprocity. These strategies are more likely seen in cults and are more linguistically sophisticated as they use things like covert hypnotic language patterns that bypass the conscious mind with positive, negative, reinforcement such as giving praise then subtly undermining it. (e.g., "You're amazing… for someone who usually messes things up"). Covert suggestions are planting ideas subtly, (e.g., "Most people wouldn't understand us like you do"), then reframing and contradiction to redefine your truth, using their narrative. ("You're not anxious, you're just afraid to be seen"). They use language saturation such as repetition, cadence, circular logic and speed (rapid fire) to overload critical thinking. These techniques create a reality distortion field. Over time, even highly intelligent, grounded individuals begin to doubt what they once knew about themselves. Why? Most people, especially empaths, don't enter relationships skeptical. We don't expect that love could be a psychological weapon. We trust words.

We trust people, and that trust becomes the very thing that blinds us to manipulation. Before the dark contract is ever signed in adulthood, the script is often written in childhood not just by our fathers or mothers but by the stories we were told about love.

In Disney films, in the pages of fairytales and later found in movies we learn of a tall, dark and seductive archetype the evasive, brooding, brilliant, emotionally unavailable man, draped in sarcasm and shadow. He is difficult, emotionally unavailable, dangerous and blurs the line between confidence and abuse.

We are made to feel sorry for his wounds while his boyish charms keep him looped in the cycles of misogyny and an insatiable need to bed as many conquests as he can because his poor ego can't trust anyone who can love him enough to save him from himself. Then he chooses you, finally, and it means you were the one. The one who unlocked him. Who saved him. Who stirred the sleeping softness in the beast. "The glorification of male emotional aloofness and volatility has long been a staple of Western media, conditioning viewers to interpret danger as depth and volatility as romantic tension." (Gilligan, C. (*In a Different Voice*, 1982).

This archetype is the cultural haunt of Beauty and the Beast, Mr. Darcy, Heathcliff, Edward Cullen, Christian Grey, not men but shadows in masculine form, projected by a society that equates unpredictability with passion, and chaos with authenticity. These men are not safe, but they are scripted to be soulmates. "Popular narratives often frame love as the ability to redeem a wounded man, a narrative that reinforces women's self-worth as rooted in caretaking and suffering. "Hooks, B. (*All About Love: New Visions,* 2000) So the trauma-bonded woman, the empath, the one with the absent, rageful, or emotionally distant father, already knows this dance. She has been trained to equate inconsistency with intensity, control with care, and neglect with need. She doesn't just fall in love, she recognizes him. The storm. The silence. The signal to earn love by staying, healing, enduring. To leave chaos would feel like betrayal because somewhere, this was called *forever*. This is the real *first* contract. The soulmate illusion, penned in projection and tied with the ribbon of a wounded inner child who once loved a man that hurt her. A father. A fantasy. A familiar ache mistaken for intimacy. "When the father is the first violator, it warps the daughter's internal compass, danger and desire become fused, and her threshold for suffering mistaken for strength." (Herman, J. (*Trauma and Recovery*, 1992).

We should have been raised on stories of Inanna, Durga, Isis, or Oya, Kali or Yemanja, the goddesses who command life, death and rebirth. Instead, we are fed the fragile myth of the princess as a passive beauty whose only value is in being seen and saved, a girl whose liberation depends on the very force that once imprisoned her. This is not empowerment, it is indoctrination. "Cross-culturally, mythologies once cantered powerful feminine figures, goddesses who reigned, ruled, destroyed, created. Their erasure is not accidental. It is the disarming of the feminine psyche." (Estés, C.P. (*Women Who Run with the Wolves,* 1992).

The dark contract therefore begins long before the narcissist appears. The first bedtime story where we're told that pain is proof of passion and the first time the girl learns, to be chosen, she must endure. Such early schemas normalize coercive attachment, priming individuals to misinterpret exploitation as connection and relational harm as confusion. Therefore, at the heart of narcissistic and psychopathic dynamics lies a deliberate disorientation between cause and effect.

These individuals masterfully oscillate between roles of the perpetrator when control is required and the vulnerable victim when consequences loom. This is not confusion, this is by design. This is strategy. This is the art of war. The narcissist injures you then mourns their own pain when you react. The psychopath deceives you, then accuses you of betrayal for uncovering the truth. They manufacture chaos, then position themselves at the centre of it, not as the one who started the fire but as the one who got most burned. This is only one side of the injury sword; the other side is the external re-injury.

"People rarely side with the victim. They side with the version of reality that costs them the least."

Most outsiders, friends, family, colleagues, see the effect, not the cause. If you are one of them, please read that again, it means a lot to the victim that you take accountability to stay informed, even if it's after the facts. Why, because the narcissist performs distress better than the survivor performs clarity. They cry. They appear broken. They spin a narrative that activates sympathy and heroism in the listener. The survivor, however, is often messy with truth. They're dysregulated, traumatized, contradictory and most of them weren't documenting everything for the predictive premeditative strategizing that occurs in order to win, however, the perpetrator was. The survivor thought they were just falling in love and now they're healing from a war no one saw.

The world prefers simplicity. To accept the survivor's story would require others to revise their own beliefs about the perpetrator. That's threatening. That takes work. So, the world often reinjures the survivor by offering them doubt wrapped in kindness: *"Are you sure that happened?", "They were always good to me.", "Maybe you're overreacting."* These statements are not neutral. They're a form of collective gaslighting, born not from malice, but from the human need to protect comfort over truth. In some cases, trained friends or family members or those with previous lived experiences are silent witnesses to someone they love entrapped in the Nex. To witness someone you love entwined in a dark contract with a narcissist, a psychopath, or any architect of confusion is to feel helpless in slow motion. You see it. Not just the person they're with, but the look in their eyes, the shrinking, the deterioration, the rationalizations, the dimming of their light and the tired hope. You've lived this before, perhaps with a partner, a parent, a sibling, and now it plays out again like a haunting, but you're not the one inside. You're the witness. The one awake. The one triggering at every micro expression, you see it all so clearly, but you are in a paradox. To intervene too forcefully is to risk becoming the threat, but to stay silent is to watch them suffer even if they don't know it yet, they feel it. So, how do you hold both love and wisdom without being pulled into the wreckage? Do not become the rescuer. The instinct to save is strong but dark contracts are built on the foundation of disempowerment, control and the illusion that others are a threat to the deep bond shared.

So, the victim is constantly checking in to prove they are following their rules. Rescuing someone risks reinforcing that very dynamic, it places your name on that threat list. The person must choose themselves, to see, to name, to leave. You can offer reflection not direction, curiosity inquiry not command. "It sounds like you're walking on eggshells a lot. How's that feeling for you?" "You don't seem like yourself lately. I miss your light." These are lanterns, not lighthouses. You shine the way, but you don't drag them to shore. Dark trait individuals often isolate their victims by seeding doubt: "They're jealous of us." "They don't want you to be happy."

If you push too hard, too soon, you risk being recast as the problem, through projection, transference, or manipulation. So instead of confrontation become a safe tether. A presence that doesn't demand or diagnose but remains open, quietly consistent. When the mask drops, and it will, they need to know there's still someone standing on the other side of the fog. Bearing witness to someone else's entrapment can retrigger your own trauma. You may feel pulled back into emotional roles you worked hard to escape, protector, peacekeeper, parentified child. This is not your contract to break. Guard your boundaries. Limit enmeshment. Take breaks. Speak with someone who can hold you as you hold space for them.

"You can care deeply without carrying entirely." (Levine, P. (2010). *In an Unspoken Voice*). Speak to the part of them that remembers. Even if they're not ready to see the full truth, they know, somewhere beneath the denial. Speak to that part. The part that's aching. Confused. Tired. Remind them, gently, who they are outside the contract. You are their mirror. Their memory. Their tether to truth and when they are ready to sever the contract, you are the soft landing on the other side.

"You don't have to decide anything today. I just want you to know, if it ever feels too heavy, you don't have to carry it alone."

So, this book is an x-ray. It is designed to expose the skeletal frame of these dark contracts, how they are created, why they work, and what part of us unconsciously signs them. These contracts are never just about them. They are about what we have yet to examine in ourselves. The Nex is not the relationship itself. It is the psychological tether that remains after logic says you should have walked away. It is what makes you stay when your boundaries are being violated. It is the script you follow without ever being told to because something in you has been trained to equate attachment with obligation, love with sacrifice, and intimacy with appeasement. In legal terms, a contract binds two parties to mutual obligations. In the Nex, this principle is subverted: one party (the dark triad personality) retains all the power and benefit, while the other (the victim) is systematically conditioned to provide compliance, empathy, resources, and loyalty in return for intermittent reinforcement a psychological principle studied in behavioral science. This is not accidental because the Nex is engineered. In the early stages, the Nex looks like a soulmate-level intensity with instant connection or obsession, excessive flattery, gifts, promises and conversations that feel "fated" or "otherworldly". This intensity is not intimacy, it is immersion. It is designed to bypass your boundaries and disarm your nervous system. You don't walk into the Nex. You are lured. Narcissists, psychopaths, and machiavellians use hidden contracts because consensual power is too vulnerable for them. They do not negotiate. They recruit. They mirror your desires so precisely that you surrender before you realize there was a battle. What they seek isn't connection, it's access. To your energy, your attention, your mind and your body. They extract and consume, but to do so, they must first gain your trust. So they disguise control as chemistry, dominance as destiny and obsession as care. Why are some of us more susceptible to these dark contracts than others? For many, empathy wasn't a gift, it was a survival strategy. In early environments marked by emotional volatility, neglect, or narcissistic caregivers, many children learned that their safety depended on how well they could read a room, soothe an adult, or disappear their own needs. What psychologists have called the fawn response (Herman, 1992; Walker, 2013) is not just people-pleasing, it is a form of hyper-attunement to threat.

Empathy becomes overdeveloped, not because the individual is naturally saint-like, but because they were conditioned to use compassion as currency. Children who experience emotional neglect often become adults who equate love with labor. As Gabor Maté (2011) notes, these individuals carry a "compulsion to self-betray" in the name of belonging. Their boundaries are porous. Their nervous systems are wired not for intimacy, but for vigilance. Narcissists, machiavellians, and psychopaths intuitively recognize this and exploit it. Victims of these dark contracts are often high in affective empathy, they don't just understand others' feelings; they absorb them (Breen & Holyoak, 2020). Without a scaffold of self-protection or secure identity, this trait becomes a blade turned inward. It's not uncommon to hear a survivor say: "I could feel their pain more than my own." Dark triad personalities use hidden contracts because explicit control would reveal their intent and strip them of plausible deniability. These individuals possess a constellation of traits that make them particularly effective at crafting unconscious bonds because narcissists demand admiration and obedience but lack true reciprocity. They use charm, entitlement, and subtle punishments to extract devotion. Machiavellians manipulate through strategy. They observe your vulnerabilities and exploit them to ensure compliance without confrontation. Psychopaths lack remorse and operate with calculated detachment. They can imitate empathy without ever experiencing it, making them lethal social predators. These traits are often cloaked in charisma, competence, or even spiritual language.

    The Nex is not always created by monsters. Sometimes, it is crafted by people who present as evolved, intuitive, or "healing." Beneath the veneer however lies a core absence of relational responsibility. To them, people are not partners, they are instruments. The hidden contract is simple: You will give. I will take. You will call it love. I will call it control. Why do we Sign the Invisible contracts? The truth is, we don't consciously sign these contracts. We inherit them. Most victims of the Nex come with a history, often developmental, often relational that predisposes them to confuse exploitation with intimacy. In early childhood, if love was earned through performance, silence, compliance, or emotional labor, the nervous system learns to associate connection with cost. This is not weakness, it is adaptive survival. What makes the Nex so potent is that it speaks directly to these unresolved internal patterns. It does not demand submission, it mirrors your unconscious programming, making it feel like home. In that sense, the Nex doesn't just trap you, it reflects you. Not the whole of you. Not your truth. But the parts that were conditioned to disappear, in order to be seen. This is where the contract finds its glue, in the unresolved longing for repair. You may unconsciously believe that if you can just love this person enough, fix them, redeem the relationship, or sacrifice more, you will finally be enough, and the pain of your past will be resolved in the present. Trauma cannot be healed in repetition only in rupture.

 A dark contract is not overt. It is drafted in subtext, sealed by self-abandonment, and upheld through psychological coercion. These are contracts that sound like; "Your needs make you difficult." "If you leave, you'll never find anyone else who understands you." "You're too sensitive. You're overreacting." "After everything I've done for you, you owe me." More subtly, they sound like nothing at all because you've internalized the contract so deeply you police yourself. You apologize before speaking. You withhold your truth to maintain harmony. You ignore your instincts to preserve attachment. You internalize their gaslighting and gaslight yourself. These contracts are invisible until named, and naming them is an act of cognitive liberation. Perhaps the most difficult truth is this, to break the Nex, we must confront our own shadow. Jung described the shadow as part of the psyche we disown. In this case, it may be the part of us that is afraid to be alone. The part that equates rejection with annihilation. *The part that still believes it must earn love through suffering.* Dark triad personalities activate this shadow in us not because they want to heal it, but because they can weaponize it. This activation is also a threshold. It's a point of choice. A place where we either double down on the pattern or there is a taboo few dare to name that runs deeper, that some part of the abuse felt exciting. Not safe, not good but intoxicating. The dark magnetism, confidence, the sharp dominance, that commanding presence, felt sexy. For survivors, especially those with high openness, emotional sensitivity, and erotic imprinting through trauma, this creates internal war. These are the deeper disowned parts of the psyche that carry repressed desires, shame, rage, and taboo.

    In the Nex, these shadows aren't just triggered, they're stimulated. Survivors may begin to associate power with pleasure, control with sexiness, and cruelty with charisma. This isn't pathology, it's conditioning. When dominance is paired with intimacy, or danger with validation, the nervous system creates a neurochemical bond (dopamine, oxytocin, cortisol) that confuses arousal with attachment and abuse with erotic charge (Van der Kolk, 2014; Carnes, 2001). This is not about consent. It's about how trauma reshapes attraction. And unless we face these shadows with maturity and non judgment, they rule us from the dark. This validates a deep human truth we may eroticize our wounds. Through conscious shadow work, we can unhook attraction from pain, passion from chemical addiction and reclaim love without distortion. Psychoanalyst Jacques Lacan offered a provocative term that speaks directly to the hidden seduction of staying bound to what harms us: *jouissance*. Unlike ordinary pleasure, *jouissance* is an ecstatic excess, a pleasure so intense it borders on pain. It is not the enjoyment of what feels good, but the compulsion to circle back to what confirms our core wound. A dark intimacy forms between the survivor and their suffering. The wound becomes a home. *Jouissance* is a pleasure that exceeds limits, transgresses norms, and borders on agony.

It is not pleasure as relief, but pleasure as return, return to the scene of the original injury, to the rhythm of rejection, to the structure of longing. *Jouissance* is the mind's way of clinging to what once hurt us, because that pain shaped who we became. The rage feels righteous. The retaliation feels like power. The fantasy of revenge tastes like a banquet, even if no one is fed and still the self is starving. Because what's being pleasured in these moments is not the present self, but the unconscious compulsion to *re-feel what we could not feel then*. At least we feel. To stay in *jouissance* is to stay shackled to the dark contract not just with the narcissist or psychopath, but with the version of the self who needed them to feel real, to feel alive, to feel *something*. Breaking the dark contract and the threads to the nex requires more than no-contact. It requires renouncing the *pleasure of the pain itself*.

This is perhaps the most difficult unbinding to let go of, the familiar ache, and risk stepping into a world where pleasure is not linked to suffering. (Lacan, J. (1998).)(Lacan, J. (2007). On the flip side of pleasure in suffering and its undercurrent of conditioning, is the archetype of the martyr, not as a formal diagnosis but it can overlap with traits from several of the dark triad's personality spectrum. Predominant in woman and or spiritual types of narcissistic personality is the covert narcissist or communal narcissist. (1. Durvasula, R. S. (2019).

This type appearsself-sacrificing but covertly manipulates through guilt, obligation and seeks admiration through *suffering*. The pain becomes a performance; "Look how much I endure for others. "There's often a hidden expectation: *You owe me, you should notice,* or *I suffer more than anyone else"*. Martyrdom may also carry histrionic features: dramatizing one's pain, needing to be seen, and deriving identity from emotional excess.

They frequently publicize their suffering, create crises, or centre themselves in others' pain. Martyrdom is often more prevalent in women, but not necessarily because of innate personality traits. It's largely cultural and patriarchal conditioning. Women are often taught to sacrifice, nurture, endure, and put others first, or risk being called selfish, cold, or "not feminine."

Religion and media can romanticize female suffering, the *good mother, the long-suffering wife, the silent daughter*. As a shadow identity it's a way of making oneself important through pain. It can reflect, repressed resentment or unmet needs. A survival strategy from childhood (being useful = being loved). A distorted sense of worth tied to suffering, and sometimes narcissistic or histrionic defences and or traits. (Gebauer, J. E., Sedikides, C., Verplanken, B., & Maio, G. R. (2012).)(Brene Brown, (2010).

Reflection Box:
- **Where do I confuse intensity with intimacy?**
- **What aspects of power or control feel arousing, yet dangerous?**
- **Do I feel shame around what part of the abuse felt "charged"?**
- **What parts of me crave power, but fear embodying it?**

Shame is formed by the illusion of consent that lives in the cognitive dissonance of abuse. We are taught that if we said "yes," it was consent. That if we stayed, it was choice. That if we signed the contract, we must have read it. When it comes to Dark Contracts, the kinds signed under duress, confusion, fear, unconscious patterns and or attachments or love addiction, consent is not consent at all. It is coercion in disguise. What Is Consent, really? Legally, consent must be freely given, informed, enthusiastic, ongoing and reversible.

Psychologically, consent must occur in the presence of, full access to one's nervous system and intuition, absence of threats, manipulation, or fear and the capacity to say *no* without consequence. Spiritually, consent is an energetic agreement of mutual presence and attunement, given in alignment with one's will, soul, and boundaries. Ethically, consent cannot coexist with power imbalance, fear of abandonment, or psychological manipulation. If you had to betray yourself to keep someone else, you were not consenting, you were surviving. Dark contracts are built on coercive control. Coercive control is a pattern of ongoing psychological manipulation, isolation, intimidation, and micro-regulation that erodes a person's autonomy and sense of self without always leaving visible marks. Unlike single or situational acts of abuse, coercive control is chronic, invisible domination, it traps the victim in a reality where consent, freedom, and identity are gradually dismantled over time.

Every Dark Contract begins with a charm offensive, not a threat. You are idealized, mirrored, flooded with attention and false intimacy, and slowly, subtly the contract is slid across the table of your psyche. You sign it without realizing that the terms will shift, that your voice will disappear, that love will become a form of psychological surveillance. You don't say yes to abuse, you say yes to connection, to safety, to hope and that "yes" is used against you until it becomes your shackle.

Many survivors often carry shame, "I should have known.", "I let them in." "I said yes." Your "yes" was not a soul consent, it was a trauma-informed compliance. It was a nervous system override. It was your inner child begging not to be abandoned again, and no law, no therapist, no God/Goddess worth invoking would call that consent. This is the Truth You

Deserve to know. You didn't agree to be discarded. You didn't choose to be erased. You didn't sign up to be punished for loving too deeply. You were coerced. Spiritually. Psychologically. Financially. Physically. Emotionally. Reclaiming your power begins by saying: "That was not consent. That was coercion, that was betrayal, that was deception, that was captivity."

Chapter Two: Dark Contracts

*"What hurts most is not the betrayal.
It's the fact that some part of you still wants to be held
by the hands that crushed you."*

Research supports that dark triad traits are dimensional, not categorical. That is, they exist on a continuum from mild to extreme expressions, rather than being "on or off" disorders (Paulhus & Williams, 2002; Jones & Figueredo, 2013). Individuals may show traits without meeting criteria for a full personality disorder, and these traits can fluctuate depending on environment, power, and perceived reward.

Low-level traits may include charm, confidence, and strategic thinking. Mid-level traits may involve deceit, emotional coldness, or egocentrism and high-level traits manifest as cruelty, exploitation, and remorseless harm. There are polarized archetypes, monsters versus mystery in our collective understanding of who and what dark triads are, most of which tend to lean into the extreme opposite end of the spectrum. At one end of the spectrum we see, demonization; serial killers, abusers, and predators, the archetypal "monster." On the other side we see eroticization; dark, alluring figures who embody taboo desire and dominance, the "smoky" erotic archetype. As mentioned previously this erotic-romantic lens is culturally reinforced in literature and media (e.g.,

Twilight, Fifty Shades, You), where dark triad traits are often sexualized and mistaken for depth or passion (Jonason et al., 2012). Psychologically, this reflects what Jung called shadow projection where repressed desires and fears are cast onto seductive others (Jung, 1959). The truth is trait expression varies, and not all individuals with dark triad features are equally destructive.

    Those with low narcissism may simply crave admiration. Those with moderate machiavellianism may be strategic, not sinister. Those with sub-clinical psychopathy may be thrill-seekers or CEOs, not murderers (Babiak & Hare, 2006). In relationships, severity, self-awareness, and behavioral control determine how "manageable" these traits are. For example, high-factor psychopathy (marked by lack of empathy, impulsivity, and aggression) is often unmanageable (Hare, 1999). Sub-clinical narcissists may function well socially but struggle with intimacy and accountability (Campbell & Foster, 2007). This book is directed toward the middle to upper regions of the spectrum including the Apex Predator: when all three masks merge. The apex predator is a personality so precisely constructed that it mirrors desire while manufacturing dependence. These individuals don't just deceive; they restructure your inner world, rewire your sense of reality, and build prisons from compliments and chaos. They are the architects of the darkest contracts.

Each mask in the dark triad brings its own toxin to the table: narcissism contributes grandiosity, entitlement, and a compulsive need for validation and power. "The narcissistic self-initiates a psychological pact with others: maintain my grandiosity or be punished." (Kernberg (1975). Machiavellianism adds strategic manipulation, emotional detachment, and long-game deception. "Machiavellians engineer asymmetric relationships through secrecy and power asymmetries." (Jones & Paulhus (2011). Psychopaths injects callousness, lack of empathy, impulsivity, and often, sadism. "Psychopaths mimic remorse only when it serves personal gain; otherwise, they see no value in it." (Hare (1999). When all three merge, you don't get a narcissist, or a manipulator, or a sociopath, you get the apex. They are calculated yet cold-blooded, charming yet cruel, meticulous yet impulsively brutal. Why Are They So Dangerous? The danger lies in the integration. The triadic predator charms you like a narcissist, traps you like a machiavellian, and destroys you like a psychopath, then walks away untouched. They play the long game of control, with the short game of pleasure, wrapped in the aesthetics of trust. "Individuals high in all three traits are uniquely dangerous, they charm to gain trust, manipulate to gain power, and exploit without remorse."(Paulhus & Williams (2002). The apex predator survives because they mimic humanity with chilling precision.

They read emotional landscapes like maps and then redraw them to serve their agenda. They charm gatekeepers (friends, family, therapists, colleagues) to block any escape routes. They manufacture chaos, then present themselves as the only source of order. They often rise to power in corporations, cults, romantic entanglements, or even spiritual communities. Their darkness is always masked by functionality. "High-scoring dark triad individuals excel in environments that reward competition, self-interest, and impression management." (O'Boyle et al. (2012). Research shows that dark triad traits have moderate heritability, but environmental factors, especially childhood trauma, neglect, or inconsistent parenting, play a major role in shaping expression *(Vernon et al., 2008; Gao & Raine, 2010)*. Psychopathy has strong neurological and genetic links particularly to deficits in the amygdala and frontal lobe regulation *(Blair, 2007)*.

Narcissism and machiavellianism tend to be more influenced by socialization, attachment ruptures, and power dynamics *(Campbell et al., 2010)*. It is therefore clinically supported to suggest that most individuals high in dark triad traits, especially those embodying the full triad (the hydra or apex profile) will ultimately betray you. It's not a matter of if, it's a matter of when. If there is a place, before the betrayal, before the silence, before the moment you began to question your own reality you remember, there was an unspoken agreement. Not a contract you signed with ink and intention, but a dark contract forged in vulnerability, longing, and illusion. These contracts are not made in the light of awareness, but in the shadow lands of unmet needs, trauma histories, and psychological baiting.

When we encounter dark triads, we are not simply meeting a person, we are meeting an offer. A subconscious lure cloaked in charm, intensity, and promises of belonging. Something deep inside us stirs, sometimes restless, aching, sometimes hopeful and without realizing it, we begin to negotiate away parts of ourselves in exchange for love, validation, or protection. These are not contracts made in good faith. They are covert agreements orchestrated by those who never intended to honor them. Narcissists, psychopaths and machiavellians craft these contracts with invisible ink, what you think you're agreeing to (love, safety, partnership) is not what they are offering (control, supply, domination). By the time the mask slips, the emotional hooks are already embedded. What follows is not just confusion or heartbreak, it is entrapment. A soul-level entanglement. This entrapment has a name: The Nex. We don't enter the Nex because we're weak or foolish. We enter because we were conditioned to abandon ourselves to be loved. Victims of these contracts often have a history of childhood emotional neglect, unmet attachment needs, parentification (becoming the caregiver too early) and a trauma that taught them love requires sacrifice. Studies show that individuals who were conditioned to be hyper-empathetic, especially women, are more likely to ignore red flags and internal warning signs in order to preserve the connection *(Carey et al., 2020)*. In this context, we do not see the contract we feel the invitation and confuse it for love. You hold two truths at once, that they hurt you, and that they love you.

The body knows but the brain bargains, and so the contract deepens. You begin adjusting to their moods, explaining away your pain and making room for their chaos. This isn't co-dependency, it's possession. What sustains it, what keeps you bound even when logic says to run, is the trauma bond.

This chapter peels back the layers of that bond. We'll explore how it forms, why it persists, and what makes it so difficult to break. Most importantly, we will uncover how the Nex turns emotional starvation into longing, how punishment masquerades as love, and how your nervous system gets rewired to seek safety in the very presence of danger. To free yourself, you must understand that you were never weak. You were tethered by design. Let's begin to sever those cords, thread by thread, truth by truth. Before we can break the Nex, we must understand what keeps it alive. Trauma bonding is not love, it is the chemical echo of survival, mistaken for connection. It is the pull you feel toward someone who hurts you not because they are safe, but because their chaos feels familiar. It is the invisible leash tied to your nervous system, yanking you back into a pattern even after your mind knows better. It is one of the most cunning threads of the dark contract. The term *trauma bond* was first introduced by Patrick Carnes (1997) to describe the paradoxical attachment that develops between victim and abuser, especially when the abuse is intermittent and unpredictable. The push and pull. The cruelty followed by kindness. The punishment punctuated with affection. This is no accident. It is a reinforcement loop, one of the oldest psychological tricks in the behavioral playbook.

The abuser alternates between threat and relief, creating a variable reward schedule, a system proven to be the most addictive reinforcement pattern in both animals and humans (Skinner, 1957; Schultz, 1997). Like the rat who continues pressing the lever in hopes of receiving a pellet, the trauma-bonded victim stays, hoping for the next moment of love, clarity, or safety. The "reward" is so rare, it becomes more meaningful. More precious. More worth the pain. This is the trap. Biologically, trauma bonding is reinforced by the very chemicals meant to sustain human connection. Oxytocin, known as the bonding hormone, is released during moments of closeness even after abuse. Dopamine spikes during the highs of reconciliation or fleeting affection, making the brain crave more. Cortisol, the stress hormone, floods the system during conflict, and its removal (when the abuser withdraws or "makes up") creates a powerful sense of relief. Together, these chemicals create a cocktail of confusion. The body starts to associate love with anxiety, intimacy with instability, and safety with subservience. This is why people don't just stay in abusive dynamics, *they crave them*. At the psychological level, trauma bonding often has roots in early attachment injuries. If love in childhood was earned, unpredictable, or withheld, the adult nervous system becomes wired to equate inconsistency with intimacy. As Bowlby (1988) wrote, attachment is not just a desire, it is a survival need. And when that need goes unmet, the psyche learns to adapt. You don't look for safe love, you look for *familiar* love. The abuser, especially one with narcissistic or psychopathic traits, intuitively detects this wound. They mirror your unmet longings. At first, they give you the love you were always denied, but later, they pull it away, not all at once, but in increments. Just enough to keep you reaching. Just enough to keep you hoping. In doing so, they turn your attachment wound into their weapon. The visual form of this is the cat toying with the half dead mouse, it doesn't want you to die, there's no fun in that, it wants you to struggle, it wants you to fight. There's a common question that outsiders ask trauma-bonded victims: *"Why didn't you just leave?"* This question betrays a misunderstanding of what trauma bonding is. The victim didn't just "fall in love." They were neurologically trained to equate fear with connection.

Their internal compass was rewired, not by choice, but by conditioning. Moreover, the victim often becomes invested in the illusion, the fantasy of who the abuser once was or could be again. That early version, the charming mask, becomes the hope they hold onto. *They don't stay for the abuse, they stay for the promise of its absence and the dopamine hit of release.* Layered underneath that is shame. Shame that they didn't leave sooner. Shame that they "allowed" it. Shame that they still care. The bond is maintained not just by fear, but by the hope that staying long enough, loving hard enough, will redeem the whole story.

To understand it from a different perspective, trauma bonding mirrors what psychologists have long recognized as Stockholm Syndrome, a psychological response where captives develop positive feelings toward their captors as a survival mechanism. Though originally used to describe hostages, the mechanism is emotionally identical, when escape seems impossible, the brain finds safety through attachment. The victim begins to empathize with the abuser, reinterpret harm as love, and internalize blame. It is not pathology. It is protection.

Reflection Box: Questions for Inward Inquiry

- **What was I taught about love, pain, and loyalty growing up?**
- **When was I first trained to mistake instability for passion?**
- **What does my body feel when I imagine walking away, for good?**
- **Do I love this person, or do I fear what their absence might confirm about me?**

Dark triad personalities don't trauma bond by accident. They use it as a tool of control. They love-bomb, then devalue. They idealize, then discard. They create dependency, then deny consistency. The result? You chase their approval like oxygen. Psychopaths and narcissists are not always physically violent, but their mastery of psychological warfare is precise. They isolate you, not just from your friends or family, but from your inner knowing. They create doubt, then offer clarity. They cause harm, then play Savior. They become both the illness and the antidote, the cause and effect. When you protest, they weaponize your empathy. They say, *"You're too sensitive"* or *"Look what you made me do"*. They train you to believe that their abuse is your fault and your responsibility to fix. This is not love. This is bondage. To break a trauma bond is to rewire the nervous system. This means not only intellectual understanding but somatic recovery. You cannot logic your way out of trauma, you must feel your way through it. This includes rebuilding trust in your own perception, earning to recognize and tolerate emotional discomfort without seeking external rescue, reclaiming power from the body through breath, movement, ritual, and presence while mourning the fantasy of who they were, so you can confront who they are. It is also a process of grief. Not just for them, but for the part of you that made the bond necessary in the first place.

    The child who wanted to be chosen. The healer who wanted to be enough. The warrior who stayed too long. Healing is not just breaking the bond. It is breaking the pattern. The trauma bond is the emotional bloodstream of the Nex. It explains why you stayed, why you doubted, and why leaving felt like dying. It is also where the healing begins because in understanding it, you reclaim the compass. The Nex may have been written in trauma, but your liberation will be written in truth, and you are already remembering. Leaving a narcissist or psychopath is not just difficult, it's terrifying. Not because you're weak, but because, by the time you even consider leaving your reality has been distorted. Your perceptions have been manipulated.

Most importantly, you've already been shown their wrath. The wrath of a dark triad personality when challenged, confronted, or abandoned is not mild. It is psychological warfare. If you dare to speak truth, assert a boundary, or attempt escape, the mask drops and what emerges is rage, contempt, punishment, and character assassination. The lesson is clear, do not poke the bear, so most don't. You learn the unspoken rules, stay agreeable, stay tolerant, stay small. In return, you're offered long stretches of peace, charm, and seeming normalcy. When the narcissist is not challenged, they can be strangely easy to live with, sometimes even deeply likable. If the person is a mother, a sister, or a lover, that "good version" of them becomes someone you grow to love. So, without fully realizing it, you begin to adjust. You become the emotional rudder of the environment. You discover that maintaining calm, avoiding confrontation, and keeping peace seems to work. This is not understanding, this is conditioning.

You're not choosing peace, you're swallowing your truth. You are not avoiding conflict, you are choking on reality.

Over time, this becomes embedded. You're no longer just managing them, you're reshaping yourself. Denial becomes a reflex. You begin to unsee what is in front of you. The damage doesn't stop there. You begin to mirror back the very behaviors that were once used against you. You learn strategies to survive, like gray rocking. You become emotionally flat, non-reactive, a shell, in order to avoid their chaos. While this protects you, it also begins to corrode your sense of self. You look in the mirror and see their residual influence staring back.

Then comes the most dangerous part of the manipulation, self-inversion. They accuse you of being the narcissist. Now, with your new behaviors, numbness, avoidance, and detachment, you begin to wonder, are they right? You're reacting in ways that look familiar. You're showing signs that once terrified you in them. You're surviving, but in their language. This is how the script gets rewritten. It begins with silencing your truth for the sake of peace. It ends with questioning your own identity. You have not become them, but you have been trained by them. And that training runs deep, far deeper than most realize. Trauma is layered and therefore so is it's healing. The trauma inflicted by dark triad personalities isn't just psychological, it's linguistic, energetic, existential, somatic and while psychology gives us frameworks, it is through the merging of spirituality and philosophy that we begin to touch the body's memory, the unspoken currents of betrayal, the felt sense of cruelty and incoherence, and find not only language for the chaos but the alchemy to transmute it into meaning, hope, and purpose. This felt sense of spiritual language invites us to look deeper and beyond pathology. For many empaths this is the realm that contradicts the essence of who they are when understanding the light and the dark as even in Jungian terms we accept we all have this aspect.

Unfortunately, this can create cognitive dissonance and challenges deeper concepts psychology doesn't always address like the flicker, those windows of lucidity where the narcissist or psychopath appeared real, even childlike, vulnerable. A glimpse into their soul. Many survivors of narcissistic, psychopathic, or machiavellian abuse speak of this fleeting moment, a flicker in the eye, a tremor in the voice, a softness that breaks through the mask. In that split second, they feel like they've seen the real person. A window into the soul that might have been. The part that could love. That wanted to care. That felt remorse. So, was it real? The answer is yes and no. For some dark triads, especially narcissists, there are moments when the false self slips, and a buried, injured part of the psyche makes itself visible. Not because they want to connect but because the mask faltered. That flicker is a ghost of the person they might have become. It is not a lie. But it is also not a promise. Sometimes the flicker is not a soul emerging, it's a strategy of confusion. A well-timed tear. A rehearsed apology. A moment of mirroring so accurately it breaks you open. Psychopaths and high-level narcissists are experts at mimicking emotion, not feeling it. How do you tell the difference? You don't, and you don't need to because even if the flicker was real, they still chose the mask. Let this be your anchor: "You are not here to fix flickers." You are not here to negotiate with ghosts. You are here to protect your light.

That glimpse may haunt you, but it does not oblige you. It is not your job to pull someone out of the darkness when they keep choosing to live there. You may have loved the flicker. The softness. The moment of mirroring. The glimpse of something real, something that felt like soul, but radical acceptance asks more of you. It asks you to hold that flicker alongside the full truth. That most of the person you loved had already abandoned the light. What remained was performance, mask, manipulation, and identity constructed in place of a self. While the flicker might have been a real shard of their humanity, it was not enough to build a future on. You cannot find healing inside someone who has made a home in their own denial. Your staying would not have saved them. It would have sanctioned their descent. It would have been a spiritual investment in their shadow, a willing donation of your light to someone who feeds on it without ever nourishing you in return, and so you left, not out of spite, but out of wisdom.

Healing cannot exist where falsehood is worshiped. Love cannot thrive where the soul is in retreat. The only true source of light they might ever access, however rare or remote, is through the death of the false self. A total surrender. A stripping down. A walk straight into the wound they refuse to name. For some, that journey is too much.

For them, death of the ego may be the only form of peace they ever know, but not for you. You live in the light and that is where your home and your healing have always been.

Chapter Three: The War Against Your Inner Truth

"The most dangerous predators do not kill the body. They kill the compass because it is the lifeline to your truth."

At first, you may not even notice it. A raised eyebrow when you recall a detail. A scoff when you express hurt. A gentle "That's not how it happened." It's small. Dismissible. That's the point. Your internal compass, your intuition, values, boundaries, and embodied sensing, is your lifeline to truth. It's what tells you when something is off, when your dignity is being eroded, and when love is turning into manipulation. For survivors of narcissistic or psychopathic abuse, it is exactly this compass the perpetrator tries to disorient, overwrite, or destroy. Why, because if you trust your inner knowing, you will leave. You will name the abuse, reveal them to themselves and remember that's death to their ego. You will then stop playing your assigned role in their script, and that is what terrifies them most, your awakening. So, the dark triads kill the compass slowly, through gaslighting, so you no longer trust your memory, through punishment for speaking up, so you stop using your voice and through praise alternating with devaluation, so you lose clarity in your identity because to them a silenced compass makes control effortless. Gaslighting doesn't begin as fire. It begins as a flicker. A subtle reshaping of your reality until you're no longer sure what's real. Gaslighting is a psychological manipulation tactic in which a person causes someone to question their own perception, memory, or sanity.

The term originates from the 1944 film Gaslight, in which a husband dims the lights and insists nothing has changed, slowly driving his wife to doubt her reality, but this is not fiction. For many who fall into the Nex, gaslighting becomes a daily psychic erosion. Unlike lying, which is overt, gaslighting is insidious. It doesn't just tell you that you're wrong, it makes you believe that your very capacity to know is broken. The gas lighter wants more than to control the narrative. They want to own your perception.When you are consistently told that your reality is incorrect, especially by someone you love or trust, your brain adapts. It de-prioritizes your internal signals in favour of external cues. This is called externalized self-referencing, and it's a known cognitive pattern in victims of long-term psychological abuse (Freyd, 1996). In time, the victim develops what researchers call betrayal blindness, a form of adaptive amnesia where the brain suppresses information that would threaten the perceived safety of the relationship (Freyd, 1999). The result? You begin to doubt your own memories. You gaslight yourself.

Gaslighting also targets the hippocampus, the brain's centre for memory and integration. Under chronic stress, hippocampal function is impaired, causing memory fragmentation anddisorientation (McEwen, 2007).

The more confused you are, the easier you are to control. In the context of the Nex, gaslighting is not just a strategy, it is a contractual clause. It reinforces the unspoken agreement: "Your truth is invalid. Mine is the only one that matters." The dark triad personality needs this distortion to maintain control. If you trusted your perception, you would see the abuse. If you trusted your feelings, you would leave. So instead, they surgically dismantle your internal feedback system. They become the narrator of your story. They rewrite timelines. They edit conversations. They reframe your reactions as irrational, your boundaries as attacks, your needs as flaws. If you protest? They call it drama. The goal is not just control. It's invisibility.

The gaslighter wants your truth so buried, so eroded, that it becomes easier for you to abandon yourself than to confront them. Gaslighting phrases sound like this; "you're too sensitive", "you're remembering it wrong", "it was just a joke", "you always make everything about you", "you're imagining things", "everyone else agrees with me", "you're overreacting." Each phrase seems minor, until you hear them every day. Then they become a spell, a slow incantation that dulls your clarity and convinces you that your reality is defective. There's a deeper level to this distortion, less studied but deeply felt. Energetic gaslighting occurs when your intuition tells you something is off, your body contracts, your chest tightens, your nervous system flares and yet the other person insists everything is fine. You feel the rupture, but they refuse to name it, and so, you begin to mistrust your own energetic signals. This internal dissonance causes what somatic therapists call neuroception conflict, when your body perceives danger, but your conscious mind overrides it (Porges, 2011). Over time, you no longer trust your gut.

You disconnect from your body. You default to their version of reality because yours has been systematically invalidated. Cognitive dissonance is a war between knowing and surviving. You didn't ignore the red flags because you were naïve. You ignored them because two truths were fighting for dominance inside you. One said, something is wrong, this feels unsafe, this doesn't line up. The other said, but they love me, I need them, I've invested too much, they can't be that bad. This is cognitive dissonance, the psychological conflict that arises when we try to hold two opposing beliefs at once. It creates an unbearable pressure in the psyche, one that intelligent, insightful people are not immune to. In fact, the more emotionally attuned you are, the more creative your mind becomes in trying to resolve that tension. So, we rationalize, excuse, or distort to make the pain feel coherent, because *certainty, even if it's false*, feels safer than chaos. The dissonance lives in the body long before the mind can name it. Your gut tightened. Your chest closed. Your heart pulled away, but your head negotiated. This is the war between the three brains: head, heart, and gut. The gut brain felt the danger. The heart brain mourned the disconnection. The head brain went into overdrive to keep the story alive. When your logic clashes with your intuition the nervous system survival wins.

Survival often means staying, smoothing over, making it make sense, even when nothing about it was sane. You didn't stay because you didn't know, you stayed because knowing would have broken the structure you were taught to build your identity on.

Reflection Box: Reclaiming the Compass

- **When did I begin to doubt my own reality?**
- **What stories did they rewrite, and which ones did I accept?**
- **What does my body remember that my mind was taught to forget?**
- **Can I begin to trust the small knowing again?**

Gaslighting does not erase the truth. It buries it in silence, where it festers until you are no longer sure if the wound was ever real. Recovering from gaslighting is not simply about "seeing clearly", it is about retraining the mind-body connection. Critical thinking, the ability to analyse facts, question assumptions, and assess patterns objectively, is systematically dismantled in Nex dynamics. Dark triad personalities don't attack your logic directly, they overwhelm it with emotional chaos, urgency, and moral ambiguity.

You begin to think in circles. The mind, flooded with cortisol and trained to prioritize emotional survival over intellectual reasoning, begins to defer. You stop thinking critically not because you can't but because the cost of questioning becomes greater than the comfort of complying.

Reflection:

What thoughts have I stopped questioning because it kept the peace?

Healing from gaslighting is not just remembering what happened. It is re-becoming the narrator of your life.

The most painful part of being gaslit is not the manipulation itself, it is that part of you allowed it. That part of you that deferred to someone else's truth over your own.

Reflection box:
- **To heal, you must meet the shadow of that part.**
- **The part that feared being "too much."**
- **The part that was taught it was safer to stay silent.**
- **The part that learned doubt was more acceptable than defiance.**

When we confront this shadow, we don't punish it, we free it. Gaslighting is the quietest cruelty. It leaves no bruises, only confusion but if confusion is a prison, then clarity is its key. By reclaiming your inner truth, you tear a hole in the Nex. You disrupt the dark contract by remembering you saw it. You felt it. You know it happened. From that small opening your voice returns. It's easy to shame the part of you that stayed. The part that excused. Explained. Betrayed yourself to stay connected to someone else, but that part wasn't weak. That part was trying to keep you safe. That part learned early that survival meant attaching at any cost. It was shaped by childhood patterns, nervous system imprints, unspoken family rules. It believed fiercely, that to be alone was more dangerous than to be disrespected. So, it adapted. It disconnected from your instincts. Not because it didn't care but because it cared too much. It needed love so badly it was willing to sacrifice truth to get it. Healing that part doesn't begin with confrontation. It begins with *compassion*.

Ask:

- **What did this part believe would happen if I walked away?**
- **Who did this part learn to please?**
- **What was it trying to protect me from?**

This is not a part to punish. It's a part to reclaim, because once it feels safe enough to stop performing, it becomes one of your most powerful protectors. Not from others, but from never abandoning yourself ever again.

Chapter Four: The Collapse of Identity

"To steal someone's power, you don't need to kill them. You only need to convince them they never had any."

To lose our identity is to lose our power, not the kind that dominates but the kind that inhabits. The power to know who you are, to feel yourself from the inside out, to choose, to say yes or no without fear. This power lies not in our titles or achievements, but in the subtle architecture of the self, the fascia of our being, the neural pathways that fire with truth, the quiet knowing that says, I exist. When bound to a narcissist or psychopath, this power is not ripped from us, it is slowly siphoned, drop by drop, through confusion, coercion, and contradiction. Over time, the self becomes porous. We adapt. We fawn. We forget. Until one day, we look in the mirror and cannot find the face beneath the performance. This chapter is a return to that face. A reclamation of the power that never truly leftbut was buried beneath the wreckage of who we were told to become.

One of the most disorienting aspects of surviving a dark contract is this quiet but devastating realization, you no longer recognize yourself. It doesn't happen all at once. It happens slowly, subtly, like erosion. A preference surrendered here. A truth muted there. A boundary softened, a voice swallowed, a dream delayed. Until one day, you look in the mirror and see not a person, but a performance. A version of yourself shaped by fear, reaction, and the desperate hope for peace. This is not just emotional pain. It is identity trauma. According to developmental psychology, identity is formed through a lifelong interplay between internal experience and relational feedback (Erikson, 1968; McAdams, 1993). In early childhood, we build our sense of self through mirroring: the emotional responses we receive from caregivers teach us who we are. When those reflections are inconsistent, conditional, or manipulative, our core identity forms around adaptation, not authenticity. Survivors of narcissistic abuse often describe feeling like they were slowly erased. That's because dark triad personalities, especially narcissists, operate through projective identification. They assign you roles based on their internal needs, then reward or punish you depending on how well you perform for them (Klein, 1946; Ogden, 1982). You become the caretaker. The mother. The confessor. The scapegoat. The mirror. In doing so, you lose the original self. Enmeshment is a form of relational dysfunction in which boundaries between two individuals become blurred or non-existent (Minuchin, 1974). In an enmeshed dynamic, the victim no longer experiences themselves as a distinct being. Their emotional state is dictated by the abuser's. Their choices are filtered through the fear of conflict or rejection.

In the Nex, enmeshment is intentional. It begins with love-bombing, idealization, and intensity. "We're soulmates," they say. "We're the same." It feels intoxicating, but it is identity fusion masquerading as intimacy. Psychologically, identity fusion is dangerous because it bypasses critical thinking. You begin to see their needs as your purpose. Their moods as your fault. Their chaos as your responsibility. Once you are fused, they can fracture you. Dark triad abusers are masterful at manufacturing shame. They make you question not only what you did, but who you are. Each criticism becomes a chisel. "You're too emotional." "You're selfish." "You always make it about you." "You're broken." Eventually, you internalize the accusation. You begin to shape your behavior not around your values, but around their triggers. You censor yourself pre-emptively. You adapt before you're asked to. You abandon your needs, then feel guilty for having them. This chronic suppression leads to what trauma researchers call identity confusion, a disintegration of coherent self-perception, often seen in victims of prolonged psychological abuse (Herman, 1992). The loss of identity is not just cognitive, it is somatic. Your body keeps score of every self-betrayal (van der Kolk, 2014).

 Over time, survivors report symptoms like numbness or dissociation, chronic fatigue or collapsed responses, muscle tension around the jaw, chest, or gut, difficulty making decisions, even small ones, or a haunting sense of unreality or depersonalization. These are not signs of weakness, they are signs of fragmentation of a self that has been overwritten too many times. At the beginning, it feels like love. They reflect the most radiant version of you, the version you've longed to become. Their gaze lands on your beauty, your brilliance, your uniqueness. It doesn't just validate you, it elevates you and, in their admiration, you begin to invest, commit to this version of you that is glowing. This is the seduction of the narcissistic mirror. It feels like a co-creation, a divine synergy between who you are and who you could be. They don't just love you, they awaken you, or so you think. You start to shape yourself around the reflection, not because you're weak, but because it feels collaborative, like you're building something luminous together. You blossom under their attention, mistaking their interest in investment, but slowly, silently, and with devastating precision, the mirror begins to shift. The light in their eye's dims. The compliments curdle. The reflection that once made you feel chosen now begins to unravel you. They say: *"You always say you're strong, but you're really not." "You're beautiful... but in a way that's fading"."You talk like you're free, but I know you, you always come back."* These aren't just criticisms. They are curses, delivered like passing remarks, but

designed to seep under your skin like spells. Narcissists and psychopaths are linguistic sorcerers. They don't wound you with fists. They fracture your identity with words. You think: "They see me. They get me. They make me better." So, you begin to trade. A little boundary here. A little value there. A small silence. A quiet override of your intuition. It's the currency of your identity being gambled on the mirage.
You think you're evolving. You think it's intimacy. But what's really happening is erosion. As time passes, the reflection begins to shift. Their gaze hardens. The compliments become double-edged. The same mirror that once lit you up now dims you down. They start to highlight your flaws, but not just casually. They curse you with words that cast spells. "You say you run, but you never do. Not really." "You look young sometimes, but also kind of... old." "You're pretty, but you've put on weight." "You act strong, but you're so reactive." These aren't observations. These are incantations. Linguistic hexes designed to break your self-trust, your image, your ground and so you adjust again, you try harder. You work to win back the original reflection. It never returns because it was never about who you were, it was about who they needed you to be to feel powerful. This is how identity dissolves, not in one moment, but in a thousand tiny, glittering cuts. Until one day, you look in the mirror and no longer recognize yourself. The face is yours,

but the fire is gone. You stopped taking photos, the dulling of the light in your eyes reminds you of the hollowing in your body, even you can see it, felt it not. The story of you has been rewritten by someone who never truly loved you, they only valued the version they could control. They didn't destroy you. They disconnected you from yourself.

Reflection Box: Coming Back to the Self

- **What parts of myself did I silence to stay in the relationship?**
- **What dreams, desires, or needs did I minimize?**
- **How often did I second-guess myself in their presence?**
- **If I removed their voice from my mind, what would mine say?**

Healing from identity collapse is not about "reinvention." It's about reclamation and reconciliation on your terms. The self you lost is not gone, it is buried, waiting to be reanimated. This is slow work. Sacred work. This is deep work. You will grieve the version of yourself who tolerated it. You will rage at the one who shaped it and then you will stand up and remember your name. What makes the collapse of identity so insidious is that it is often voluntary, at least at first. You handed over parts of yourself in hopes of peace, love, or the unconscious reconciliation of a wound from the past that craved healing. In the Nex, identity is not taken violently. It is borrowed slowly. One sacrifice at a time. One silence at a time, but what was taken can be remembered. What was buried can be restored and what was erased can rise again, louder, wiser, whole. You have an original blueprint, and it is uniquely, wildly, wonderfully, yours.

Chapter Five: The Dark Lure of Power Reversal

"Holding onto anger is like drinking poison and expecting the other person to die."

Buddha

After the gaslighting, after the trauma bonding, after the collapse of self, something stirs. Something long buried. Not grief. Not fear. Rage, and with it, the fantasy: what if I could make them feel what I felt? What if I could turn the tables? What if I could be the one who walks away first, for once? This is the revenge fantasy, a psychological coping mechanism, a stage of reclamation, and a dangerous crossroads.

When a person has been chronically disempowered, manipulated, and emotionally violated, the desire for revenge is a normal and adaptive response. In fact, research in affective neuroscience shows that imagining revenge activates the brain's reward circuits, including the caudate nucleus, which is associated with planning and executing goal-directed actions (de Quervain et al., 2004). In short, the brain experiences imagined revenge as a kind of victory. It's the mind's way of reclaiming power when real-world justice feels unavailable, but there's a difference between feeling the fantasy, and feeding it.

From a Jungian perspective, the revenge fantasy is a projection of the Shadow Self, the part of us that contains the repressed emotions we are socially or morally taught to disown (Jung, 1953/1968). Rage. Hatred. Cruelty. Dominance. These are cast out of our conscious self-image, especially if we see ourselves as kind, empathetic, or peaceful. When we are violated and powerless for too long, the shadow breaks through. It does not ask for permission. It arrives with flame in its teeth. The fantasy of retaliation is not inherently toxic, it is a signal that a boundary has been broken so deeply that the psyche can no longer hold the pain without imagining inversion. Left unchecked, the fantasy can become fixation and fixation can become behavior, and in that moment, you risk becoming the very thing that harmed you. For many trauma survivors however, anger is not just dangerous, it was forbidden. In homes or relationships marked by volatility, cruelty, or emotional neglect, expressing anger often led to punishment, abandonment, or escalation. So, the body adapted, and it learned to fawn, to be hyper-nice, to become the emotional thermostat of the environment. These survivors were praised for being "mature," "selfless," or "so well-behaved", when in reality, they were children carrying the weight of other people's dysfunction. Anger wasn't absent, it was buried, denied, pressed deep into the fascia, the nervous system and the gut. Over time, what was emotional becomes physical, headaches, digestive issues, chronic back pain, even autoimmune conditions. The rage doesn't disappear, it implodes, it becomes cellular. That's why expressing anger is not optional, it's imperative.

It doesn't require the abuser's presence, validation, or participation. Anger can be ritualized, written, roared into pillows, danced out of the bones, or woven into a new contract, one in which the survivor no longer absorbs harm, but names it, unbinds from it, and reclaims what was stolen. Anger anesthetises giving you leverage to cope at your pace. It can also be transmuted, directed into a powerful energy that elevates you out of the ashes. It's important to know however the distinction between the anger you use and the anger that uses you. Dark triad personalities provoke retaliation deliberately. They want to provoke your rage, so they can point to it and say, "See? You're the abuser." This is called reactive abuse, when the victim lashes out in desperation or survival, only to have that reaction used as evidence against them (Forward & Frazier, 1997). It's a trap. The Nex doesn't always end when the relationship does. It persists in these cycles of revenge, obsession, and imagined retribution. You think you're reclaiming power but you're still in the dynamic.

Still tethered. Still spending your energy on them. In this way, revenge becomes another thread in the contract. A darker one. A sharper one. But still a bond. The desire for retaliation is also rooted in the body. When a trauma survivor finally moves out of freeze, they often enter fight, a state of mobilized energy, anger, and survival assertion (Levine, 1997). This is a healthy stage of trauma resolution. But if this energy has nowhere to go, if it's not witnessed, expressed, or processed, it can turn inward or outward as destructiveness. Inward becomes shame, self-harm, dissociation and outward becomes obsession, revenge-seeking, even stalking or counter-manipulation.

There comes a point in the survivor's journey when the script flips, when you look back on your outbursts, your screams, your breaking point, and you realize, it was orchestrated. You get pushed beyond human limits and lash out emotionally, verbally, or physically. Dark triad personalities use strategies like gish galloping, a rapid-fire of accusations and distortions that overwhelm your ability to think or respond rationally (Brandolini, 2013). They weaponize your vulnerable truths, as things you once whispered in trust are now hurled back as ammunition. They stonewall or bait by alternating silent treatments and antagonism to destabilize you emotionally. They want you to lose it. They want you to yell, cry, or hit back, because when you do, they can flip the narrative, and you become the abuser. They become the misunderstood victim, and your credibility begins to erode, internally and socially. This serves several functions for the perpetrator; Control, by destabilizing your emotional regulation, they assert dominance over your reality. Plausible deniability, they can deny their actions and point to your reactions as the "real problem." Isolation, others see your breakdown, not the manipulations that preceded it, pushing you further into silence and shame. According to trauma psychologist Judith Herman (1992), repeated psychological violations create a state of "learned helplessness" and emotional flooding, where the victim is neurologically overwhelmed. In that state, breakdown is inevitable, and the abuser knows it, but here's the truth, your reaction was not proof of your toxicity. It was proof of your breaking point, and they pushed for it with precision.

Recognizing reactive abuse for what it is does not absolve you of responsibility, but it restores context, compassion, and clarity. It reminds you that your reaction was engineered, and that your work now is not to stay silent, but to heal the nervous system that was pushed into collapse. (Brandolini, A. (2013). Brandolini's Law, also known as the Bullshit

Asymmetry Principle.) (Herman, J. L. (1992). Trauma and recovery: The aftermath of violence from domestic abuse to political terror*. Basic Books.) The work, then, is not to suppress this rage but to use it, transmute it and ritualize it. Give it form and release without destruction.

Reflection Box: Meeting the Vengeful Self

- **What does my revenge fantasy want me to feel?**
- **Where in my body do I hold the desire to punish?**
- **What would justice feel like if it didn't include harm?**
- **How can I acknowledge my rage without being consumed by it?**

Retaliation is seductive because it feels like power. But true power is the ability to walk away without needing the last word. Revenge is not evil. It is honest. It is the body's cry for power after too much powerlessness. To act on it blindly is to bind yourself to your abuser's vibration. To process it, name it, and release it? That is alchemy. The Nex can be broken with fire, but only when that fire is contained, witnessed, and transformed.

Chapter Six: Soul Theft

*"Some losses cannot be named in language.
Only in silence. In the hollow that remains when something sacred has been taken."*

You left the relationship. Maybe months ago. Maybe years, but still, you feel them. In your dreams, in your nightmares. In your body. In the way you hesitate to speak too loudly or take up too much space. You deleted their number. Blocked their accounts. Burned the bridge, but something remains. A psychic tether. A fog. A depletion you can't explain. This is soul theft, the final thread in the Nex, and perhaps the deepest. Soul theft is not a clinical diagnosis. It's a term used to describe the deep energetic depletion, disconnection, and disorientation survivors often feel after enduring prolonged psychological, emotional, and relational abuse, especially in relationships with narcissistic, psychopathic, or machiavellian individuals.

In trauma psychology, it mirrors what Judith Herman (1992) called a loss of selfhood, or what Janina Fisher (2017) refers to as self-alienation, when parts of the self are exiled, hidden, or split off as a survival mechanism. In somatic terms, it may feel like depression, chronic fatigue, numbness, or dissociation, emotional flatness or apathy, difficulty making decisions or knowing what you want, stuttering, foggy brain, forgetfulness, feeling like you're no longer inside your body and a strange, persistent sense that "something is missing" soul theft is not metaphor. It is a nervous system that has been colonized. A body that has been trained to serve someone else's needs, moods, and expectations until it forgets its own. Dark triad personalities don't just manipulate emotions. They embed themselves in your psyche and energy field through repeated mirroring, trauma bonding, boundary violations, and inconsistent reinforcement. This creates an energetic cord, what some refer to as a psychic hook, an enmeshment, or a sympathetic tether.

While not always part of traditional psychotherapy language, these concepts map onto known psychological patterns like co-dependency, enmeshment, and internalized object relations (Kernberg, 1975). In simpler terms: they get in you. And after they leave, they stay. Not physically, but energetically, like a shadow embedded in the fabric of your being. Survivors often describe a haunting emptiness, a hollow ache where something used to live. It's not just heartbreak. It's soul theft, the felt sense that some vital essence was swallowed by the relationship, siphoned out through coercion, or emotional enmeshment. This is no metaphor. It's an imprint. Their energy lingers like a parasite, feeding off memory, shame, longing, and unresolved pain. The narcissist or psychopath installs themselves inside your nervous system.

From a neuroscience perspective, prolonged relationships with narcissistic or psychopathic individuals activate the stress response system, especially the hypothalamic-pituitary-adrenal (HPA) axis, leading to cortisol dysregulation, adrenal fatigue, and eventual emotional shutdown (McEwen, 2007; van der Kolk, 2014). You're not just tired. You're systemically drained. Chronic hypervigilance, masking, and self-suppression eventually wear down the brain's ability to regulate emotion, memory, and attention. The prefrontal cortex dims. The limbic system overreacts or underreacts. Your sense of self, housed in the interweaving of neural and somatic pathways, becomes blurred. In trauma recovery, this is often referred to as soul loss, not in a religious sense, but in the loss of wholeness, coherence, and vitality. Beyond the body and brain lies something harder to define but no less real, the loss of meaning. When someone has taken your trust, distorted your memories, colonized your identity, and exhausted your energy, what remains? Often, nothing feels real. Your memories feel fogged. Your past feels foreign. Your future feels unreachable. This is what philosopher Martin

Buber called I-It relating, a dehumanizing dynamic where you become an object, not a subject, in someone else's story (Buber, 1923/1970).

The Nex strips you of your I, leaving you floating in someone else's projection. It is existential theft. And recovering from it is not just therapy, it is soul retrieval. "They didn't just hurt you. They hollowed you. The healing begins the moment you decide to return to your own body, your own voice, your own name." The return to self must be intentional.
This is not just about trauma recovery, it is about re-embodiment, ritual, and sovereignty.

Reflection Box: The Soul's Return

- **Where do I feel most absent from my life?**
- **What did I abandon in myself to survive the Nex?**
- **What would it mean to reclaim my presence, fully?**
- **What rituals help me feel wholewithout apology?**

The Nex does not just break hearts, it breaks presence. It pulls you out of your own life, leaving you sleepwalking through someone else's design. This is one of the deepest ruptures a soul can endure, the psychic death that occurs after the rupture of an illusory, narcissistically bound reality. What you're describing isn't just grief. It's an existential collapse, the kind that splits the self at the level of identity, future, memory, and meaning. There is a moment when the Soul Splits. To the observer you can see it in their eyes. To the receiver it's a jolt that forces you out of your slumber as you suddenly view the death of Illusion.

That exact second when you realize they were never who you thought they were, and in that moment, something more than the relationship dies. The future you planned is gone. The version of you who believed in it is shattered. The dream, the home, the laughter, the language, the shared toothbrush drawer, dissolved. Even time becomes slippery, memories now feel contaminated, unretrievable, suspect. This is soul detachment. Not just heartbreak but the dislocation of identity from meaning.

You wake up in a world that is still spinning, but none of it feels like yours anymore. So how do you recover when the loss isn't just of a person, but of yourself? You begin by naming the Deaths. You must grieve what died. Not just "the relationship," but each layer of it. The death of the imagined future. The death of shared friends and family. The death of financial security. The death of innocence of the belief that love always saves. The death of trust in your own perception. The death of the self you once were. Write them out. Speak them aloud. Mourn them individually. This is a ritual of psychic burial, and it is necessary. Chunk the Collapse into more malleable forms bit by bit. Your nervous system cannot metabolize the total loss all at once. So, you must chunk the grief, one memory at a time. Let the photos hurt. Let the song break you. But not all at once. One loss at a time. Mourn the home today. Mourn the trust tomorrow. Mourn the "what could have been" next week. You do this to survive the immensity. You do this to keep your soul from scattering further. Reintegrate the Soul through witness. A trauma like these needs witness not advice.

Find someone who can sit with your story without minimizing, spiritual bypassing, or comparing. Whether it's a therapist, a trauma-informed friend, or a mirror you cry into, your soul needs to be seen to return to you. What was broken in relationship must also be healed in relationship. Let the Self reemerge from the rubble. You do not return to who you were before them. That version of you is gone. You do not stay in exile either. A new self emerges, like the phoenix, built not on illusion but on self-reverence. The self that comes next no longer seeks salvation in someone else but is now cantered in their truth. This is rebirth. Not replacement. You will love again not because you forget. Not because you regress, but because you learn that real love doesn't mean abandoning yourself. You

will love again but first you must become the beloved of your own soul. You didn't just lose a partner. You lost parts of yourself buried in memories, objects, traumas, and empty promises.
So now, the work is to call them home, and when the final piece returns, sometimes in a dream, a breath, a sunrise, in music, in dance, in nature, or a poem, you will feel it; the spark of the rejoining and the sacred yes of coming home to yourself.

Chapter Seven: The War Between Knowing and Denial

"I knew and I didn't know. Somewhere between the two, I lost myself."

There's a particular kind of torment that lives in the space between conflicting truths. You know you were hurt, but you remember how they held you. You know it was abuse, but you can still hear their voice in your head, saying "You're overreacting." You know you need to leave, but your body aches at the thought of goodbye. This is not confusion. This is cognitive dissonance, the psychological clash that happens when two opposing truths both feel real, and for those entangled in the Nex, it is not just a mental discomfort. It is a fracture. Coined by social psychologist Leon Festinger (1957), cognitive dissonance is the mental distress that occurs when a person holds two or more contradictory beliefs, values, or perceptions at the same time. In abusive relationships, especially those built on gaslighting and trauma bonding, cognitive dissonance becomes chronic. One part of you sees clearly. The other part still hopes, still defends, still denies. Over time, the internal tension becomes unbearable. And instead of confronting the abuser, the victim often doubles down on the illusion, because that feels safer than facing the truth. Cognitive dissonance is not just psychological, it is somatic. Polyvagal theory (Porges, 2011) teaches us that the nervous system is constantly scanning for cues of safety or threat. But in dissonant environments, the signals are mixed. The body says danger, but the abuser says love. The heart says run, but the brain says wait. This creates what therapists call a rupture between what is felt and what is allowed to be known. The result is dissociation, emotional paralysis, chronic indecision and internalized self-blame. The body holds truth, but the mind is trained to suppress it. The body always knows.

Long before the mask slips or the chaos begins, the body whispers what the mind has been trained to dismiss. A tight chest during a charming apology. A wave of nausea after an intense confession. A shallow breath as they subtly undermine you. The body is often called the subconscious because it stores what words can't name, and speaks through sensation, not logic. In the early stages of any relationship, those cues are there. But we don't listen. Not because we're weak but because we're strong. We say: "It's nothing," "I can handle this," "Everyone has flaws," or "I've been through worse." Our resilience becomes our override system. We keep going not because we're naïve, but because we are resilient. We mistake the body's warning for anxiety, or trauma talking, or our own baggage and in doing so, we override the truth. The body never lies, if it feels wrong, it is. Denial is not ignorance. It is protection. The victim is not blind, they see the red flags.

They feel the pain, but to fully acknowledge it would require the collapse of the entire relational fantasy and with it, the self-image they constructed inside that fantasy. So, the psyche bargains. It rationalizes. It reframes the abuse as love, the cruelty as stress, the manipulation as trauma they couldn't help. Hope becomes a drug. A veil. A survival strategy, but hope, when used to bypass truth, becomes another strand in the Nex.

Reflection Box: Naming the Split

- **What did I know but push away?**
- **What internal signals did I ignore to stay in the story?**
- **How did I keep the illusion alive and what did it cost me?**
- **What truth do I already know, but haven't yet made peace with?**

"Cognitive dissonance doesn't mean you didn't know. It means part of you did and part of you was silenced."

Dark triad personalities thrive in dissonant space. They want you confused. Confusion creates compliance. They say

"You're the only one who gets me" right after blaming you for their breakdown. They say "I never meant to hurt you" right after violating your boundary. They praise your sensitivity and then call you unstable. They oscillate between idolization and devaluation with such precision that your nervous system begins to distrust clarity itself. This erosion of inner coherence is the real damage.

Once you stop trusting your own perception, the Nex doesn't need to bind you. You'll bind yourself. The path out of dissonance is not immediate clarity. It is integration. You do not need to cancel the part of you that loved them. You need to hold that love in the same hands that hold the truth: They harmed me. This means allowing conflicting truths to coexist without rushing to resolve them, speaking what you knew even when it's uncomfortable, forgiving yourself for the ways you silenced your knowing and rebuilding coherence through somatic practices, narrative reprocessing, and relational repair. You do not need to choose between knowing and compassion. You only need to stop abandoning yourself in the name of someone else's comfort. The hardest part of cognitive dissonance is the realization that you betrayed yourself to keep the peace. You quieted the truth. You gaslit your instincts. You dimmed your rage and dressed it in forgiveness.

Leaving a narcissist or psychopath is not just difficult, it's terrifying. Not because you're weak, but because, by the time you even consider leaving, they've already trained you. Your reality has been distorted. Your perceptions have been manipulated, and most importantly, you've already been shown their wrath. The wrath of a dark triad personality when challenged, confronted, or abandoned is not mild. It is psychological warfare. If you dare to speak truth, assert a boundary, or attempt escape, the mask drops and what emerges is rage, contempt, punishment, and character assassination. You learn strategies to survive, like grey rocking. You become emotionally flat, non-reactive, a shell in order to avoid their chaos. You adapt because resistance invites punishment. While this protects you, it also begins to corrode your sense of self. You look in the mirror and see their reflection staring back as the lines blur between your authentic self and the persona you had to wear to stay safe.

Then comes the most dangerous part of the manipulation: self-inversion. They accuse you of being the narcissist, and now, with your new behaviors, numbness, avoidance, and detachment, you begin to wonder, are they right? You're reacting in ways that look familiar. You're showing signs that once terrified you in them. You're surviving, but in their language. This is how the script gets rewritten. It begins with silencing your truth for the sake of peace and it ends with questioning your own identity.

    Rest assure you have not become the narcissist, but you have been trained by them. That training runs deep, far deeper than most realize. To heal, you must face this, not with shame, but with reverence, because that self-betrayal wasn't weakness, it was survival. Now, your task is to return. To gather all those fragmented parts and make them whole again. Accepting its new form, guarding it by internalizing all that love you were seeking. Cognitive dissonance is not a flaw. It is a fracture born from being asked to hold the impossible. You did not lie to yourself. You simply weren't ready to hold the full weight of truth. But now you are. Now you see. Now, the war inside you can end by choosing to become, again.

Chapter Eight: Ghosted by the Living

*"They were still breathing beside you,
but you could feel the absence like a death."*

There is a kind of silence that doesn't mean peace. It means obliteration. It means you're speaking, but no one is listening. It means you're touching someone whose spirit has already left the room. This is what it feels like to be ghosted by the living. Not because they disappeared physically, but because they were never present. They systematically, repeatedly discarded you emotionally, psychologically, spiritually over and over and now they're just waiting for the final exit. This is the most shattering stage of the Nex: the devaluation and discard phase. It is not just a breakup. It is a psychological disintegration, a collapse of connection, identity, and coherence and it often happens without a word.

In relationships with dark triad personalities, especially narcissists and psychopaths, idealization quickly gives way to devaluation. What was once praised is now picked apart. Your sensitivity becomes "too much." Your independence becomes "selfish." Your needs become "needy." This devaluation is a calculated form of control. It prepares the ground for discard, the final act in a cycle of emotional conquest. According to the cycle of narcissistic abuse (Brown, 2009), the discard phase is not necessarily permanent, it may be followed by hoovering or intermittent re-engagement, but it always leaves a deep psychic rupture, because the discard is not just rejection, it is erasure. Psychologically, discard triggers what attachment theorists call abandonment trauma, especially for individuals with early attachment wounds (Bowlby, 1988). But this wound is often compounded by gaslighting, trauma bonding, and identity erosion that came before it. You are not just being left. You are being left by someone who once mirrored your soul. You are being left without explanation, accountability, or closure. The human brain is wired for narrative coherence (McAdams, 2001). When there's no explanation, the mind fills in the blanks, usually with shame; "I wasn't good enough.", "If I had done more, they would have stayed." "It must have been my fault." This shame is not logical. It is embodied, and it makes the discard phase far more devastating than a mutual breakup or clean ending. It doesn't just rupture your heart. It implodes your story. To discard someone, you must first stop seeing them as a person. That is exactly what happens in the Nex. Dark triad personalities operate through what object relations theorists call splitting, they see others as either "all good" or "all bad," with little room for complexity (Kernberg, 1975). When the victim no longer reflects their idealized image or begins asserting needs, boundaries, or autonomy, they are recast as "bad," disposable, unworthy. You are no longer a subject. You are an object.

Not a person with feelings, but a tool that no longer functions. Not a partner, but a reflection that cracked, and in that moment, the discard is not just cruel, it is dehumanizing. This shift from idealization to devaluation is not merely interpersonal; it is *ontological (at the core of your being)*. It erases your personhood. What follows is not a typical relational rupture, but a psychological dismantling. The abuser's gaze flattens, no longer registering you as a subject with interiority, but as an obstacle to be removed or a defect to be punished. This is where many begin to experience a deep, pre-verbal dread, a somatic knowing that they are no longer seen, but surveyed, no longer loved, but assessed and in that surveillance lies the first flicker of something colder than neglect, a stark, cold, calculated detachment that preludes the full emergence of malevolence. Psychologist Dr. Jordan Peterson has stated that one of the most disturbing experiences a person can have is to come face-to-face with true malevolence, a person so devoid of empathy, so calculated and emotionally cold, that their presence evokes a visceral, biological alarm. It's a palpable, haunting feeling. A kind of body-level knowing that something ancient and unsafe stands in front of you. Survivors often describe feeling lightheaded, breathless, or suddenly nauseous in the presence of these individuals because the nervous system is reading something the mind hasn't yet processed, you are in the presence of the predatory. Peterson describes this recognition not as logical, but existential. A soul-level confrontation with the reality that evil exists, not as an idea, but as an active force.

When a dark triad individual drops the mask, even for a second, this feeling floods the body. I am not dealing with someone who is simply wounded, I am dealing with someone who is dangerous. This highlights a clear psychological and emotional transition between dehumanization and the visceral recognition and warning of danger. One collective recognized sign of this darker sadistic or confronting trait is the chilling micro expression reported by survivors, the smirk. It's a fleeting, involuntary half-smile that appears in moments of emotional cruelty. Often seen during discard, invalidation, or emotional injury, this smirk isn't misinterpreted. It is an artifact of contempt. According to Paul Ekman's research on micro expressions, the smirk is a universal facial marker of dominance, superiority, and sadistic satisfaction (Ekman, 2003). It's not easily detected consciously, but for trauma survivors, especially those with a history of early relational danger, the body often perceives it before the brain catches up. Many survivors of narcissistic or psychopathic abuse report that they "felt" something shift, a sense of pleasure in the abuser's face during moments that should have been solemn or remorseful. The smirk reveals the game, the win. It confirms the manipulation. And while the logical mind may override it, the body stores it. These micro expressions become part of the survivor's post-traumatic hyper-awareness that hauntingly replays over and over, reinjuring the point of entry to the worst part of the wound.

Reflection Box: Facing the Ghosting

- **How did they begin to emotionally exit before they physically did?**
- **What explanations did I create to avoid facing the truth?**
- **What part of me still waits for a goodbye that may never come?**
- **What does my grief need in the absence of their accountability?**

"Being discarded doesn't mean you were unlovable. It means they couldn't love anyone beyond the mask."

Being ghosted by the living is not just a psychological event, it is an energetic shattering. You shared your soul, and now, there is a sudden vacuum. A withdrawal so complete that it feels like a spiritual blackout. Some survivors describe this as psychic shock. In Jungian terms, it's the death of a projection, the moment you realize the person you loved never truly existed as you imagined (Jung, 1953/1968). This grief is not just about them. It is about the version of you that lived inside that dream. The most dangerous part of the discard is the way it lures you back in, not to them, but to the idea of them. You search for meaning. You revisit messages. You over-analyze. You replay it all, hoping to find the one moment where you could've changed the ending, but there was never going to be a soft landing. Closure will not come from them. It will come when you stop needing the story to end differently. That's when integration begins. That's when you stop trying to fix the past and start reclaiming the present. To heal this phase, you must grieve the ghost without re-haunting yourself. Reclaim your narrative without their validation. Restore your presence in the now, where they no longer belong and sit with your grief without bargaining with the past. This grief is sacred. It marks the death not just of a relationship, but of a contract you never consented to and in its place, something new can be born. To be discarded without explanation is a violence of all that you are. It says: "You are not even worth an ending." That is a lie.

You were never discarded because you were unworthy. You were discarded because your presence threatened the illusion. You saw them, and that is death to their ego. When the victim no longer reflects their idealized image or begins asserting needs, boundaries, or autonomy, they are recast as "bad," disposable, unworthy. You are no longer a subject. You are an object. Not a person with feelings, but a tool that no longer functions. Not a partner, but a reflection that cracked, and in that moment, the discard is not just cruel, it is dehumanizing. What follows can be even more wounding, there is a second rupture.

A collective one. The re-injury of group betrayal happens when shared friends, allies, and even long-time supporters turn away, not just silently, but sometimes aggressively. They side with the abuser. They echo the narrative. They exile you. Why, because you became a threat to the illusion.

You were a threat to the image they share, the comfort they protect, the memories they share, the future they plan and the stories they tell themselves about who this person is. So, they choose harmony over truth, control over compassion and preservation over justice. This betrayal is not just social, it is soul dismemberment. You, the victim, loses everything. The person you loved, the shared home, routines, conversations, the future you planned, the identity you formed, the friends you laughed with, the extended family who once embraced you, the safe spaces you trusted, the version of reality you believed was true. Each loss is a death and all at once, it is too much for the nervous system to hold. This is why survivors of narcissistic and psychopathic abuse often report symptoms akin to complex PTSD, betrayal trauma,and disassociation. (Freyd, 1996; Herman, 1992). Exile isn't just relational. It's existential. Surviving the Systemic Loss requires honoring the loss, reconnection to a new community, somatic body practices and finding meaning in your suffering. (Frankl, V. E. (1959). Freyd, J. J. (1996). Ogden, P., Minton, K., & Pain, C. (2006). Porges, S. W. (2011).

DARK CONTRACTS BY DEIRDRE ROLFE

Chapter Nine: The False Resurrection

"They come back not to love you but to see if they still can."

Just when you begin to breathe again, when the fog lifts, when the silence becomes peace instead of pain, your phone lights up. A message. A memory. A song you once shared posted to their story. A sudden apology. Or worse, something vague: "I've been thinking about you." "Can we talk?" This is not a miracle. It is not growth. It is hoovering, the psychological vacuum that tries to suck you back into the Nex. Hoovering is a manipulation strategy used by narcissistic, psychopathic, and emotionally predatory individuals to re-engage a former target after the discard phase. The goal is not reconciliation, it is reinstatement of control.

Named after the Hoover vacuum, this behavior is meant to pull you back in just enough to re-establish their energetic dominance over you. It is rarely about real repair. It is about power. Hoovering can take many forms: Sudden apologies or declarations of love. Nostalgic messages designed to trigger longing. Playing the victim to elicit guilt or rescue. Accidental or "coincidental" encounters. Indirect contact through mutual friends or social media. Cryptic or vague gestures meant to reignite your curiosity. What makes hoovering so potent is its timing, it often arrives at the moment you're beginning to heal, reclaim your power, your finances, your integrity and self. That most certainly is not an accident. It's design. To understand hoovering, we must return to the psychological structure of dark triad personalities. At the core of narcissism and psychopathy is entitlement without empathy (Hare, 1991; Millon et al., 2004). These individuals do not see people as autonomous beings but as extensions, utilities, reflections. When you disengage, you're not simply leaving. In their mind, you are malfunctioning. You were supposed to stay bound to the role they cast you in. So, when you start healing, when your glow returns, when your clarity solidifies, they sense the shift. Not intuitively, but tactically. Your energy, your silence, your absence, it triggers them. Not because they love you, but because they are losing their grip on the emotional leash and so, they come back. Not with truth but with bait. Even after all the hurt, a hoover can light something up inside you, perhaps it's hope, longing, the fantasy of closure, the aching desire for an apology that might finally feel real. This is not weakness. This is neurobiological conditioning. The trauma bond, coupled with intermittent reinforcement (Skinner, 1957), wires the brain to stay alert for reward. That reward may be a compliment, an explanation, a breadcrumb of remorse. When it comes, the dopamine hit feels like love, but it is not love. It is addiction to the illusion and the moment you respond, the cycle begins again.

A vital and nuanced concept is that going back to the narcissist isn't just about craving the reward of affection or approval, it's often about relief from pain, especially pain caused by the bond itself. Psychology and trauma research help us understand this through the lenses of addiction, intermittent reinforcement, attachment trauma, and nervous system dysregulation. In abusive dynamics, especially with narcissists, survivors often return not because they believe the abuser has changed, but because the pain of separation becomes intolerable. The trauma bond creates a biological dependency, where the nervous system becomes hooked not only on the emotional highs but also on the temporary relief from the lows. This mirrors addiction as the survivor isn't chasing a healthy connection, they're trying to escape withdrawal. Psychologist B.F. Skinner found that unpredictable rewards are the most addictive. Narcissists use this by alternating love and punishment, creating emotional gambling machines. When survivors return after hoovering, the short burst of warmth or validation relieves anxiety, shame, and despair even if it's short-lived. (Reference: Skinner, B.F. (1953). Science and Human Behavior.)

If a survivor has an insecure or disorganized attachment style (often from childhood trauma), they may associate love with anxiety, inconsistency, or fear. The narcissist mimics these early patterns, reawakening the body's learned need to "fuse" with the source of pain for safety. Going back temporarily regulates the survivor's dysregulated nervous system but only because it relieves the very pain the abuser caused. (Reference: Schore, A.N. (2003). Affect Dysregulation and Disorders of the Self.) (Reference: Levine, P. (2010). In an Unspoken Voice: How the Body Releases Trauma and Restores Goodness). Returning to the narcissist brings a surge of soothing chemicals, not because the person is safe, but because the addiction to relief has taken hold. (Reference: Carnes, P. (1997). The Betrayal Bond: Breaking Free of Exploitive Relationships.) Returning to the narcissist isn't just about craving the next high, it's about escaping the unbearable low their absence leaves behind.

Reflection Box: When They Come Back

- What do I want from their return? And what have they offered?
- Do I want healing, or do I want validation?
- Who am I trying to redeem: them, or the part of me that stayed too long?
- What has healed in me that they are now trying to interrupt?

"They don't return because they miss you. They return because your silence became louder than their control."

Hoovering is dangerous because it doesn't just re-engage the relationship, it resurrects the version of you who was bonded to it. The moment you respond, even out of curiosity, the inner architecture of the Nex begins to rebuild. You begin doubting yourself again. You shift attention from your own growth to their intent. You abandon the present to revisit a carefully curated past. You split into two selves: one who knows better, and one who still hopes. This false resurrection of the connection can delay healing for months, or years. It keeps you orbiting their gravity instead of stepping fully into your own. The hoover is not love's return. It is the final temptation to stay asleep, but you have already awakened. You can't unseen them now. So, all that's left is to walk forward and never answer when the past calls pretending to be the future.

When a narcissist or psychopath threatens harm as you're leaving, or even within the first few years after, the threats can be both strategic and real and it's critical to take every threat seriously, no matter how manipulative it seems. Studies on intimate partner violence and coercive control (Stark, 2007; Herman, 1992) show that the most dangerous time in an abusive relationship is the moment of leaving or shortly after. This is when the perpetrator feels the greatest loss of power and may lash out. So, are the threats Real or are they just strategy? They can be both. Some are psychological warfare to get money, control, or legal wins but some are deadly real, and it's impossible to know which until it's too late. Golden Rule: Assume every threat is serious until proven otherwise. Strategic Threats (Control, Court, Money) are often to intimidate you into staying, gain leverage in legal battles (e.g., child custody, property), punish you emotionally for asserting independence or to scare you into silence or submission. Common manipulations: "I'll take the kids, and you'll never see them again." "I'll ruin your reputation." "You'll end up broke and alone."

These are coercive control tactics meant to activate fear, guilt, and compliance. Real and Dangerous Threats are often when they feel they've lost control, their public image is threatened, they're exposed or facing consequences or they have nothing left to lose. Red flags for Real danger: a history of violence or cruelty, stalking, surveillance, or property damage, sudden obsession with your movements, threats of "If I can't have you, no one can", owning weapons or mentioning specific plans. According to Dr. Robert Hare and others who study psychopathy, individuals high in these traits lack remorse and can escalate unpredictably when their control is challenged. Do Not Negotiate with your safety. There comes a moment when you are feeling, uncomfortable and sacred and angry but you must decide, your safety or your survival. The shattered fragments of who you used to be, realizes they've taken everything.

    Many survivors stay not because they love the abuser, but because they fear the unknown, the financial instability, the systemic injustice, the loneliness, the weaponized reputation damage that begins the moment you break their rule and that fear is valid. These are not normal endings. These are exits from a dark contract, signed under duress, sealed by manipulation, and enforced by fear.

    Fear is a chain and negotiating your life in exchange for temporary certainty is the currency of entrapment. If you stay because you fear losing your home, your income, your stability, you are paying with your mind, your body, your health and your essence and there is no greater currency then that. You are investing in slow death. There is no paycheck in the world worth the erosion of your essence. So, you must learn to not equate money with safety, justice or integrity.

    Psychopaths and narcissists know exactly how to structure the scene. They leave you out of documents, position themselves as the "provider," while you unknowingly provide the invisible labour. When it comes time to leave, the paper trail betrays you because they built it to. You were busy surviving while they were busy planning. Most survivors lose everything, money, mutual friends, community, identity and still have to carry the burden of looking like the one who "walked away." But what you walked away from was annihilation, even if the court doesn't recognize it, your nervous system does. Justice isn't always linear. This is the hardest part because they may appear to get away with it.

They may win in court. They may keep the house, the car, the children, the lie. They may remarry within months and mimic the same story you lived. They may post their new life, rebranded and rehearsed and you're left with the wreckage.

Let this be known however, no one gets away with who they are. The bill for harm always comes due. Sometimes quietly, sometimes publicly, but always eventually. Even those who side with them feel it. They know. The mask may not slip in court, but it slips behind closed doors and in the patterns. They all have a timeline of bitches, assholes and psychos behind them, over time it's clear who the common denominator is. Truth needs no audience. So, if all you have left is the truth you carry, let it be enough. It may not feed you, but it will free you. It may not win you allies, but it will return you to yourself and that is the first form of justice: the return. The full reclamation of who you were before they colonized your confidence and branded your worth.

Let the world spin how it spins. Let the lies run their course. Let time take care of what the courts could not. You, beloved, are the one who got out and that's what they'll never get over.

Chapter Ten: The Shadow You Stayed For

"The power you thought they stole was never theirs. It was only waiting for you to remember where you buried it."

You survived. Not just the discard, the gaslighting, the soul-theft but the slow, agonizing unravelling of who you thought you were. You looked into the abyss, and though it looked back, you didn't fall in. You're not who you were before the Nex. You never will be, but what rises now is not a return, it is a becoming and it begins with power. True power is the reclamation of agency. The authority to name your reality. To own your story. To choose your path without apology. It's not about control over others. It's about integration of self, body, voice, instinct, shadow, and soul. The Nex fractured you. It split you between what you felt and what you allowed. What you needed and what you were told to tolerate. The healing journey now becomes a process of re-integration. This includes somatic reclamation, returning to the body with presence and authority, narrative sovereignty, writing your story without distortions or edits, energetic containment, no longer leaking power to past dynamics and digging deep into shadow integration You must meet the parts of you that stayed, tolerated, or retaliated with compassion and maturity. The unbound self does not deny the darkness. She metabolizes it into wisdom. One of the first signs of the unbound self is the shift in language: "Why did they do this to me?" becomes "Why did I stay?", "What's wrong with me?" becomes, "What in me was still unhealed?" "I can't believe they did that" becomes "I can believe it and that's why I left." This is not self-blame. It's self-ownership.The power to name your patterns is the power to break them.

"Healing is not the return to who you were. It is the rise of who you were never allowed to be."

Reflection Box: Who Am I Becoming?

- **What am I no longer available for?**
- **What did survival teach me that I now carry as wisdom?**
- **What feels like mine again—my body, my voice, my joy?**
- **Who am I when I am no longer surviving but sovereign?**

There comes a moment in the healing, not in the beginning, not even in the middle, but at the sacred edge of integration, where you no longer carry the rage, or the blame, or even the grief. It lives outside of you now. You've cried it. Screamed it. Walked it out. Written it down. You've done the layers. The work. The rage. The rituals. And then… there's silence. Not the silence of numbness. The silence of arrival. You may meet this version of yourself many times. In glimpses. In fragments. But there will be one definitive moment, the one you never forget, when you truly meet your whole self. It doesn't come in a breakthrough, it comes in a reckoning. The reckoning that there was a part of you not weak, not broken but shadowed, that linked into them. The part of you that stayed not because of trauma and not just because of fear, but because something in them called to something in you. That wanted to be heard.

You see it clearly now.

This is the final layer. The deep layer. This is where forgiveness stops being about them and starts being about you. You cannot release what you still shame. You cannot integrate what you disown. So, you must take an extra chair, sit with and meet the rebel. The risk-taker. The abandoned child. The part of you that wanted to feel alive even if it meant handing your body, your mind, your magic to someone who only mirrored you for their own survival. When you face her, (him, them). You dance, you laugh, you listen, you negotiate, you understand. You don't pretend it didn't happen. You don't deny the pain, but you learn to feed the shadow in sacred ways: Through art. Through dance. Through deep, safe intimacy. Through poetry, movement, erotic truth, wildness that doesn't destroy but liberates. You are finally free.

Not because you let go but because you looked deeper, you choose you. You are not what they did to you. You are what you chose to become after and in that becoming, the Nex dissolves. Knowledge is more than power, it is protection. In the context of narcissistic and psychopathic entanglements, knowledge becomes the sharpest tool in dismantling delusion. This book is not just a narrative of survival, it's a manual of discernment. The more clearly we understand the behaviours, strategies, and neurological patterns of dark triad personalities, the more swiftly we can recognize them and refuse the contract. Psychopaths and narcissists rely on your confusion, your hope, and your conditioning. Awareness punctures the initial attempt. Research shows that those with high emotional empathy, unresolved childhood trauma, and insecure attachment styles, especially anxious-preoccupied or disorganized, are statistically more susceptible to exploitation and coercive control (Bailey &Freedenfeld, 2020; Bowlby, 1988). When your nervous system is wired for vigilance instead of intimacy, you may overlook danger because danger feels familiar. It's not just your past that puts you at risk it's the parts of yourself you're taught to abandon. Your intuition. Your anger. Your discernment.

Many trauma survivors were conditioned to override these inner signals to maintain attachment. They were praised for being kind, forgiving, and tolerant even in the face of betrayal. Dark triad personalities exploit these very traits. They are drawn not to weakness, but to light because light is fuel. That is why it's not enough to only study them; we must study ourselves. Where do we override instinct for hope? Where do we confuse chemistry with resonance? Where do we reward charm over character? By knowing the red flags in others and the blind spots within, we become less catchable, less mouldable, less appetizing. Knowledge allows you to spot the subtle grooming, the mirroring, love-bombing, emotional enmeshment and interrupt it before it embeds. It gives you language for what once left you speechless and boundaries that are fixed not flexible, not malleable. Most importantly, it breaks the cycle.

Dark triads rarely look like monsters, in fact it is one of the most insidious realities about narcissists and psychopaths, that they rarely look dangerous. In fact, many present as successful, insightful, generous, or even spiritual. The "dark triad" when clustered together, should trigger heightened awareness around, charm, incongruency, and intensity. These individuals speak fluently in therapeutic or philosophical language. They know how to mirror your depth. They often present as emotionally articulate, even trauma informed. This triad isn't a diagnosis, it's a warning system. They are dangerous because their ability to mimic light while feeding on your vulnerability is based on their survival.

They may appear emotionally intelligent, but their empathy is often cognitive, not affective, they understand your feelings, but they do not feel them. This is where neuroscience becomes crucial, it repeats the fact so our minds can comprehend. Studies on psychopathy have shown distinct structural and functional differences in the brain, especially in areas related to emotional processing and empathy. So, for example, reduced activity in the amygdala and ventromedial prefrontal cortex, regions responsible for fear, guilt, and emotional regulationare common in psychopathic profiles (Kiehl, 2006; Blair, 2007).

This neurobiological detachment explains why they can simulate emotion without embodying it. They don't bond. They simulate bonding. And they use your longing for love as the bait. This is why intellectual insight alone isn't enough, in fact it can blind you. You must also learn to trust your body. If someone seems "too good," too synced, too fast, that's not fate it's often a strategy. The charm isn't real. The incongruency is a signal. The intensity is weaponized. Identifying these patterns, these slight distinctions, by looking for the patterns and understanding the science beneath the mask, you unhook from the myth that "if it feels deep, it must be real." You replace wishful thinking with radical clarity and radical truth. There are some lesser known but essential truths to consider; They often tell you exactly who they are, early. (Never trust someone who needs to tell you who they are to avoid you discerning for yourself.) Narcissists and psychopaths tend to confess in plain sight, through jokes, half-warnings, or bravado cloaked in charm. "I always get what I want." "You'll never leave me." "People say I'm intense but I'm just honest."

Believe them the first time. (Believe someone when they tell you what they plan to do.) They study you for use, not understanding. What feels like deep connection at the start is often strategy. They are mapping your hopes, insecurities, and soft spots not to love you, but to leverage you. They're more insecure than you think. Behind the inflated ego lies a bottomless void of shame, envy, and inadequacy. Their cruelty is not confidence, it's camouflage for collapse. They interrupt to reassert dominance. Interruption isn't just poor manners, it's a power play. Each disruption is a small act of destabilization, reminding you whose voice is louder. Remember, they watch even after you leave.

Psychopaths and narcissists often continue tracking ex-partners digitally, not from longing, but to ensure their sense of control remains intact. They create flying monkeys without trying (loyal friends who align to them). Not every smear campaign is deliberate. Their manipulative charm and victim posturing are so reflexive that people rally around them without being asked. They come in quiet, "Nice" packages too. Not all are loud or grandiose. Some are gentle, anxious, "wounded," or spiritual. It's not the tone, it's the manipulation beneath the performance. They mirror your pain, not just your dreams. What bonds you might feel like deep resonance but it's often trauma reenactment. They reflect your unresolved wounds back to you, not your soul. They discard you the moment you awaken. You think they left because you were "too emotional." In truth, they discard when your clarity threatens their control. They don't miss you, they miss the power. If they return, it's rarely about love or remorse. It's about feeding the contract again, where they were central, needed, and obeyed.

Epilogue/Conclusion

You Were Never Broken

You've made it to the final pages, not just of this book, but of a cycle. The Nex has been broken. You have seen its patterns, decoded its terms, grieved its illusions, and burned its contracts in the fire of your own truth. And through that process, something ancient returned to you. You own you: your space, your clarity, your voice, your power, your choices, your integrity and your permission to never again abandon yourself in the name of belonging. Your only sacred contract is to yourself.

I, the undersigned, now and forever revoke all unconscious contracts that required me to shrink, silence, sacrifice, or disappear in order to be loved or safe. I no longer consent to relationships, roles, or environments that require me to abandon myself in exchange for conditional acceptance. From this moment forward, I choose to live in alignment with the following truths:

1. Boundaries Are My Birthright

I recognize that my time, body, energy, and voice are sacred. My "no" is not a negotiation.

My "yes" will be given only when it honors my truth.

2. Awareness Is My Protection

I commit to listening to the signals in my body, my intuition,

and my inner voice.

I will not override red flags in the name of hope, habit, or illusion.

I will choose clarity over chaos, even when it's uncomfortable.

3. Compassion Begins With Me

I release the need to fix, rescue, or absorb the emotions of others.

I extend compassion to my past selves—for what they tolerated, what they didn't yet know, and how hard they tried to survive.

I will not weaponize compassion against myself by calling it loyalty.

4. I Remember Who I Am

I am not broken, too much, too sensitive, or difficult.

I am a whole human being reclaiming pieces that were stolen, shamed, or silenced.

I will not forget my truth to make someone else comfortable with their distortion.

5. I Live Life On My Terms

I define my success.

I choose my pace.

I set my standard for love, safety, and connection.

I am no longer available for performance-based belonging or emotionally predatory dynamics.

Signed,

Date:

This contract is not between you and the world. It is between you and the part of you that never stopped knowing the truth.

"Every time you self-abandon, silence your needs, forgive the unforgivable, and sacrifice it all, Dark Triads will reward you with calm, a fleeting sense of connection, and a few brief moments of love. They are behaviourally conditioning you to believe that love is earned through your erasure.

To heal do not look only at the symptoms of anxiety, fatigue, dissociation, or numbness as something to fix. It is a signal from your body, a message from the unconscious to ask yourself:

What is absent from my life?
What part of myself have I repressed, exiled, or abandoned in order to adapt or belong to survive?
What unlived life is haunting me?
What does this denial cost my wholeness, my individuation?
And if I were to turn toward that absence, if I were to reclaim the lost parts, how might my life begin to feel more whole, more real, more mine?"

May you never thirst!
Deirdre Rolfe xx

Reference & Book Recommendations

REFERENCES

American Psychiatric Association. (2022). Diagnostic and statistical manual of mental disorders (5th ed., text rev.). American Psychiatric Publishing.

Babiak, P., & Hare, R. D. (2006). Snakes in suits: When psychopaths go to work. HarperBusiness.

Bailey, B. E., Freedenfeld, R. N., Kiser, R. S., & Gatchel, R. J. (2003). Lifetime physical and sexual abuse in chronic pain patients: Psychosocial correlates and treatment outcomes. Disability & Rehabilitation, 25(7), 331–342. https://doi.org/10.1080/0963828021000030533

Blair, R. J. R. (2007). The amygdala and ventromedial prefrontal cortex in morality and psychopathy. Trends in Cognitive Sciences, 11(9), 387–392. https://doi.org/10.1016/j.tics.2007.07.003

Bowlby, J. (1988). A secure base: Parent-child attachment and healthy human development. Basic Books.

Brandolini, A. (2013). The bullshit asymmetry principle. [Unpublished or web-based manuscript].

Brown, B. (2010). The gifts of imperfection: Let go of who you think you're supposed to be and embrace who you are. Hazelden.

Campbell, W. K., & Foster, C. A. (2007). The narcissistic self: Background, an extended agency model, and ongoing controversies. In C. Sedikides & S. Spencer (Eds.), The self (pp. 115–138). Psychology Press.

Carey, M. A., Steiner, K. L., & Petri, W. A., Jr. (2020). Ten simple rules for reading a scientific paper. PLOS Computational Biology, 16(7), e1008032. https://doi.org/10.1371/journal.pcbi.1008032

Carnes, P. (1997). The betrayal bond: Breaking free of exploitive relationships. Health Communications.

Cialdini, R. B. (2001). Influence: The psychology of persuasion. Harper Business.

Durvasula, R. S. (2019). Don't you know who I am? How to stay sane in an era of narcissism, entitlement, and incivility. Post Hill Press.

Durvasula, R. S. (2021). Should I stay or should I go? Surviving a relationship with a narcissist (Updated ed.). Post Hill Press.

Ekman, P. (2003). Emotions revealed: Recognizing faces and feelings to improve communication and emotional life. Times Books.

Evans, D. (1996). An introductory dictionary of Lacanian psychoanalysis. Routledge.

Festinger, L. (1957). A theory of cognitive dissonance. Stanford University Press.

Fink, B. (1995). The Lacanian subject: Between language and jouissance. Princeton University Press.

Fisher, H. (2017). Anatomy of love: A natural history of mating, marriage, and why we stray (2nd ed.). W. W. Norton & Company.

Forward, S., & Frazier, C. (1997). Emotional blackmail: When the people in your life use fear, obligation, and guilt to manipulate you. Harper.

Freyd, J. J. (1996). Betrayal trauma: The logic of forgetting childhood abuse. Harvard University Press.

Gao, Y., & Raine, A. (2010). Successful and unsuccessful psychopaths: A neurobiological model. Behavioral Sciences & the Law, 28(2), 194–210. https://doi.org/10.1002/bsl.924

Gilligan, C. (1982). In a different voice: Psychological theory and women's development. Harvard University Press.

Hare, R. D. (1999). Without conscience: The disturbing world of the psychopaths among us. Guilford Press.

Herman, J. L. (1992). Trauma and recovery: The aftermath of violence—from domestic abuse to political terror. Basic Books.

Jonason, P. K., Li, N. P., Webster, G. D., & Schmitt, D. P. (2009). The dark triad: Facilitating a short-term mating strategy in men. European Journal of Personality, 23(1), 5–18.

Jones, D. N., & Figueredo, A. J. (2013). The core of darkness: Uncovering the heart of the dark triad. European Journal of Personality, 27(6), 521–531. https://doi.org/10.1002/per.1893

Jung, C. G. (1959). Aion: Research into the phenomenology of the self (R. F. C. Hull, Trans.). Princeton University Press.

Kernberg, O. F. (1975). Borderline conditions and pathological narcissism. Jason Aronson.

Kohut, H. (1971). The analysis of the self: A systematic approach to the psychoanalytic treatment of narcissistic personality disorders. International Universities Press.

Lacan, J. (1998). The seminar of Jacques Lacan: Book XX – Encore (On feminine sexuality, the limits of love and knowledge) (B. Fink, Trans.). W. W. Norton & Company.

Lacan, J. (2007). The seminar of Jacques Lacan: Book XVII – The other side of psychoanalysis (R. Grigg, Trans.; J.-A. Miller, Ed.). W. W. Norton & Company.

Levine, P. A. (2010). In an unspoken voice: How the body releases trauma and restores goodness. North Atlantic Books.

Maté, G. (2011). In the realm of hungry ghosts: Close encounters with addiction. North Atlantic Books.

Miller, A. (1981). The drama of the gifted child: The search for the true self. Basic Books.

Millon, T., Grossman, S., Millon, C., Meagher, S., & Ramnath, R. (2004). Personality disorders in modern life (2nd ed.). Wiley.

Minuchin, S. (1974). Families and family therapy. Harvard University Press.

Paulhus, D. L., & Williams, K. M. (2002). The dark triad of personality: Narcissism, Machiavellianism, and psychopathy. Journal of Research in Personality, 36(6), 556–563.

Porges, S. W. (2011). The polyvagal theory: Neurophysiological foundations of emotions, attachment, communication, self-regulation. W. W. Norton & Company.

Skinner, B. F. (1953). Science and human behavior. Macmillan.

Žižek, S. (2006). How to read Lacan. W. W. Norton & Company.

RECOMMENDED READING

Brown, B. (2010). The gifts of imperfection: Let go of who you think you're supposed to be and embrace who you are. Hazelden.

Carnes, P. (1997). The betrayal bond: Breaking free of exploitive relationships. Health Communications.

Durvasula, R. S. (2021). Should I stay or should I go? Surviving a relationship with a narcissist (Updated ed.). Post Hill Press.

Estés, C. P. (1992). Women who run with the wolves: Myths and stories of the wild woman archetype. Ballantine Books.

Gilligan, C. (1982). In a different voice: Psychological theory and women's development. Harvard University Press.

Herman, J. L. (1992). Trauma and recovery: The aftermath of violence—from domestic abuse to political terror. Basic Books.

hooks, b. (2000). All about love: New visions. William Morrow Paperbacks.

Kernberg, O. F. (1975). Borderline conditions and pathological narcissism. Jason Aronson.

Kohut, H. (1971). The analysis of the self: A systematic approach to the psychoanalytic treatment of narcissistic personality disorders. International Universities Press.

Maté, G. (2003). When the body says no: Exploring the stress-disease connection. Vintage Canada.

Van der Kolk, B. (2014). The body keeps the score: Brain, mind, and body in the healing of trauma. Viking.

Walker, P. (2013). Complex PTSD: From surviving to thriving. Azure Coyote Books.

www.ingramcontent.com/pod-product-compliance
Lightning Source LLC
Chambersburg PA
CBHW062039290426
44109CB00026B/2676